To Mom
With love and

S

D1179088

Stéphane

Darlings of
the Gods

Darlings
of the Gods

One Year in the Lives of
Laurence Olivier and Vivien Leigh

Garry O'Connor

HODDER AND STOUGHTON
LONDON   SYDNEY   AUCKLAND   TORONTO

British Library Cataloguing in Publication Data
O'Connor, Garry
    The darlings of the gods: one year in the
    life of Laurence Olivier and Vivien Leigh.
    1. Leigh, Vivien   2. Olivier, Laurence
    Olivier, *Baron*   Actors – Great Britain –
    Biography
    729'.028'0922   PN2598.L.46

    ISBN 0-340-34346-X

THE OLD VIC

THEATRE COMPANY

A
TOUR
OF
AUSTRALIA
&
NEW ZEALAND
MDCCCCXLVIII

To
Michael
Redington

CONTENTS

ILLUSTRATIONS

Between pages 80 and 81

Old Vic cargo boat[1]
Between rehearsals[2]
Under captain's scrutiny[1]
River Swan reception[2]
Belle of Atlantic City[3]
Larry for England[4]
Thespians in whites[5]
The protector[1]
Here tomorrow[6]
Strand electrics[7]
Couples must lie apart[5]
Young marrieds[8]
Eye on the ball[5]
Flirty Lady Teazle[9]
Irascible Sir Peter[3]
Beach party in Brisbane[5]
Casualty of Bosworth Field[10]
Dockyard pas de deux[2]

Acknowledgments
1. By courtesy of Mercia Swinburne
2. Photograph by Terence Morgan
3. By courtesy of John Vickers Archives
4. By courtesy of Paul Farmer
5. By courtesy of Michael Redington
6. By courtesy of Australian Consolidated Press Ltd.
7. By courtesy of Bill Bundy
8. By courtesy of Herald and Weekly Times
9. By courtesy of Floy Donnell
10. By courtesy of John Fairfax Ltd.

LADY TEAZLE'S RED SHOES

Christchurch, in spite of its old-world, cloistered atmosphere, got on their nerves. The weather blew cold and beastly. The crowds amassed again, as they had in Auckland and previously in Australia, to greet Laurence Olivier and Vivien Leigh in force outside the United Services Hotel in Cathedral Square.

"I was passing nearby and noticed a crowd gathering," recalled Shirley Piddington, a shorthand typist in the State Fire Insurance Office. "I rushed over but my view of the hotel entrance was blocked by a car which the ever-growing crowd had me pressed against. To my delight it was *their* car. Miss Leigh sat in the window leaving only the window glass separating us. She gave me the most exquisite smile which I never returned—I had just had my two front teeth removed because of an abscess."

In the meantime, Olivier, on foot, passed Mrs Piddington senior in the street. "He must have decided to walk the few blocks to the theatre, Mum said, an ever-increasing crowd following him forced him into rapid strides. He obviously arrived at his destination out of breath."

Fortunately, instead of the usual conference only one representative of the press called on him, but he then had problems with the hotel which had put him and Vivien in a room with separate single beds—he insisted they be changed for a double —and did not like having to serve them a meal after the evening performance. When they arrived at the theatre for the opening of *The School for Scandal*, another set of problems beset them. As in Auckland they played at a theatre called the St James's; but here, because of an industrial dispute, their costumes had been delayed at the wharf and were late in being unpacked. Several local girls had been pressed into helping them pile and hang clothes at the last minute, among them Barbara Packwood, a first-year student at Canterbury University.

The girls were working in the basement of the theatre when

Vivien entered, dressed as Lady Teazle but in slippers, and demanded to know where her red shoes were. The girls scurried about looking for them, but no shoes could be found.

"She stormed at us," said Barbara Packwood. "I can still see her eyes flashing—highlighted of course by stage make-up." Then in swept Olivier who demanded to know what was going on. Not seeing the girls ("we flattened ourselves against the wall"), he told Vivien she was late and had to get up on stage. She replied she would not go on without her red shoes, to which he countered, gritting his teeth, "Put on any shoes, and just get up there!" She repeated she would not go on without the shoes. According to Barbara Packwood,

> By this point they are facing each other and a great battle of wills is going on. We hardly breathed, needless to say. He slapped her face and said, "Get up on that stage, you little bitch!" She slapped his face, saying, "Don't you dare hit me, you—you bastard." He looked at her and then said quietly in his most beautiful voice, "And don't *you* dare to call me a bastard, because *we* know who is one, don't *we*," and tapped her on the nose with his forefinger. [He referred to her desertion of Leigh Holman and of her child Suzanne.] She started to cry saying, "You always throw that up at me." Whereupon he took her arm and said, "Come on, up on stage, I'll find some shoes for you," and out they went.

"Thank you for your reception," Olivier said when he spoke to the audience at the end of that first performance of their two weeks' stay in Christchurch which took place in unusually damp and cold weather. "I can see we shall be as reluctant to leave Christchurch as your nose and throat troubles are to leave you!"

Well might the Hollywood producer Sam Goldwyn have asked Olivier, as he did when he first heard about the Old Vic tour to Australia and New Zealand, "Why are you, the greatest actor in the world, taking a touring company to Australia of all places?"

PART ONE

Outward Bound

I'm looking for Elysian Fields.
Blanche Dubois in *A Streetcar Named Desire*

1 For King and Commonwealth

The advance party for the Old Vic Theatre Company's ten-month British Council Tour of Australia and New Zealand left England on the SS *Moreton Bay* on 6 February 1948: all male, it consisted of three actors, a scenic artist, a property master, a master carpenter, electrician, and the stage, assistant stage, and company managers. Sleeping four to a cabin, they found themselves among five hundred passengers, mostly children and old people. After a cold crossing of the Bay of Biscay they passed Gibraltar in the night; next morning they basked on deck on a flat, warm and sunny Mediterranean before docking at Valetta, where numerous British warships, including an aircraft carrier, stood at anchor. Some of them went ashore here, rising by lift to the town where they were stopped by many locals wanting to show them round. Wandering at will they heard weird music; they witnessed a fight of which no one took much notice; in the shops they freely bought English sweets and biscuits unobtainable at home.

Back on board, now on the Red Sea in blazing sunshine, they changed into white flannels and white shirts; they played housey-housey and deck tennis, or, feeling too hot, the card game solo in the shade of the lifeboats. The ship's doctor warned of moving about without adequate protection, and deckhands covered the chairs to stop them being stained by sweat. When, five days later, they reached Colombo the weather turned even more humid and close; some of them caught tropical diarrhoea, for which the doctor prescribed tablets. The stage manager had a lung haemorrhage and the doctor suspected T.B. The authorities had been going to put him ashore at Port Said, but his condition improved, and, by confining him to the ship's sick bay, they allowed him to continue the voyage.

Crossing the Indian Ocean on the final run of the 10,000-mile passage the advance party dined one evening at the captain's table and talked of the fancy dress parade to be held on board on the last night. They had now been at sea for nearly a month. The three actors, Michael Redington, John Barnard and Denis Lehrer, decided to go as the Marx Brothers, and won first prize although Redington, disguised as Harpo, failed to obtain a motor horn and had instead to employ a whistle.

When at last they docked in Fremantle, the seaport twelve miles south–west of Perth, their first impression was of profuse sunshine. In the light, incomparably clearer than in England, you could see for miles. Except for the suspected T.B. case—at once driven to hospital in Perth and placed under observation—all were passed by the doctor fit for disembarkation. Although in what was to follow their roles were relatively humble, they were given a hearty welcome, and pictures and interviews appeared in several Western Australian newspapers.

Ninety-seven per cent of all people in Australia at that time were of British stock, and the Labour Prime Minister, ex-locomotive boilerman Ben Chifley, had not long before, in the Canberra Parliament, singled out Australia's relations with Britain as her most important overseas interest. He exhorted his country to help her with food:

> The mother of all the British Commonwealth of nations which carried the greatest burden throughout the war and bore the greatest loss of life and suffering, came out of it the world's greatest debtor nation, although she had gone into it one of the world's greatest creditors. Do the Dominions say [to her]: "We have done well out of the war . . . you ought to be prepared to sacrifice your country so that we may continue in our money-making ways?" And again, "Australia is one of the countries which made the least economic sacrifice and suffered least in World War II. Are we to deny the United Kingdom . . . which bore the brunt . . . wheat, butter and other goods?"

The search for accommodation for the forty-odd members of the Old Vic Company had begun some nine months before, when Marie Donaldson, a tall, young and engaging New Zealand woman with strong, Spanish-looking features, set out from Christchurch where she worked in the University Library, to begin her work as PRO for the tour. Marie quickly discovered the live performer to be a breed about whom most Australians knew very little and cared even less. They were not at all prepared to accommodate the English actors, even temporarily—despite the exhortations of their own Prime Minister.

Especially in the larger cities, Sydney and Melbourne, on the Company's itinerary there seemed small hope of success in her mission and she had frequently to explain that people who made their living on stage did not observe the same hours of eating and sleeping as did ordinary folk. The actor had his or her main meal of the day at night after the show, and generally went to bed at one or two in the morning (she did not know that Vivien Leigh invariably went to bed at three or four, if at all). He rose at eleven and after a light snack did not usually take lunch or a large meal at midday, preferring—if it were free—liquid refreshment; in the afternoon he had "high tea". Such a routine was likely to turn the usual hours of hotel life upside down, especially as in working arrangements Australia, with its strong sense of regulations and its influential unions, showed little flexibility.

Marie did not lose heart, but she had to report that in the whole of Australia she found only one proprietor, a Sydney man, who professed a liking for stage people, and who would commit himself to having 25 of the company. In Perth, where she tried 22 hotels, she herself ended by sleeping in a broken-down place over the railway. Here, she declared unhappily, her room felt like an oven, and she could not bear even a sheet over her; all night she was plagued by ants and mosquitoes dive-bombing her. Running hot water did not exist, and the calefont, or geyser, over the bath had failed. The omens were decidedly poor: theatrical "digs", as such, did not exist.

The danger of lack of accommodation did not, however, apply to the leaders of the Old Vic tour. Hundreds of people wrote to Miss Donaldson offering to put them up. Apparently, a Perth columnist grumbled, it was better to be a famous actor than a returned soldier with a family, for every week soldiers came back and could find nowhere to live, while Sir Laurence and Lady Olivier had only to open their mouths by proxy, stating they wanted somewhere, and a rush of offers followed. If so many places actually were available, ominously warned the paper, some "responsible authority" ought to discover why they were withheld from families of men who had fought to "keep this country safe for the landlords and their properties".

On 14 February, as leaders of the tour, Laurence Olivier and Vivien Leigh boarded their boat train for Liverpool at Euston Station. They were waved goodbye by Messrs W. J. Jordan and J. A. Beasley, High Commissioners in London for New Zealand and Australia. It made some good publicity stills for St Valentine's Day—they relaxed easily into the role of "perfect lovers" as, her arm slipped through his, they smiled at the cameras and at each other. The station-master wore a top hat. "Many sweet people seeing us off. Many sweet fans and many sweet flashbulbs," wrote Olivier in a leather-covered diary sent by a well-wisher.

In Durham Cottage, Chelsea, the night before, they had had seventy "intimate" friends to a "bon voyage" party during which Danny Kaye gave Olivier advice: "If you prepare every speech you are asked to make you'll have a nervous breakdown. If you make enough lousy speeches—lovely! They'll stop asking you to make any more."

In the 1920s, with actors such as the flamboyant Oscar Asche, theatre had flourished in Australia. Even Shakespeare, at the Princess Theatre in Melbourne, had achieved a remarkable popularity. Gregan McMahon and Allan Wilkie presented twenty-five of his plays, making a grand total of 1,200 performances. But ten years later the story had been rather different. Economic decline and the rise of the picture palace had almost killed the live theatre. Now, after the war, only a few amateur companies operated in the big cities, though from time to time attempts were made to encourage Australian writing. Films or Variety usually filled the theatres—well-known Variety performers from abroad would visit them, and were usually supported by local talent. Although the standard of radio drama was high, for the sole presentation of stage plays there existed in the whole of Australia only the Minerva Theatre and the better known—but still only semi-professional—Independent Theatre Company, based in

North Sydney and run by the actress Doris Fitton. The acting profession remained small.

But the appetite for drama was there, and Olivier and Vivien were, they had been assured by the British Council (motto: "Truth will triumph"), certain of a rapturous welcome. When Cecil Beaton, who designed one of the productions, first went to discuss it Olivier told him, "We're banking on every performance playing to capacity." As ambassadors extraordinary for British culture, and as part of the gesture of thanks to Australia and New Zealand for their support, with men and materials, of the British war effort, the Old Vic Company could do a lot to revive ties. A further intention of Olivier's was to make money for the Old Vic which badly needed it. The present season of 1947–8 had not been going as well as those of 1944–5 and 1945–6, for which both Olivier and Ralph Richardson had been specially released from service in the Fleet Air Arm, and which had, with *Peer Gynt, Richard III, Henry IV Parts 1* and *2,* and *Oedipus* made theatrical history. In the context of his wider ambition Olivier also saw this touring company as a nucleus for the permanent company which he, Richardson and John Burrell, directors-in-triplicate of the Old Vic, hoped to establish at the Old Vic and which would, in time, lead on to the formation of a national theatre. So into the Company he had deliberately brought such rising talent as Terence Morgan, Peter Cushing and Dan Cunningham, who had all been in his film of *Hamlet,* now completed and due for release in 1948.

Yet during the weeks previous to departure Olivier and Vivien had snubbed or ducked all attempts by Australian or New Zealand interviewers to know their thoughts—or lack of them, as one of the latter ruefully expressed it—on leaving for the Antipodes. If, at such distance, their dislike of publicity was so alarmingly to the fore, how would they behave on actual arrival?

At the beginning of 1948 the lives of the two principals of the tour were on as extraordinary a plane as any two lives in this century. Not only were they known all over the world, and fêted wherever they went, but a unique additional factor reinforced their fame.

Since his film appearances as Heathcliff, Maxim de Winter, Mr Darcy, Lord Nelson in *Lady Hamilton* and, particularly, Henry V, and his stage appearances as Richard III, Astrov, Lear and Oedipus, Olivier had become widely accepted as being "the finest actor in the world". This, at any rate, was how the Company manager, Clive Woods, described him on 6 March 1948 to the press in Fremantle. Also, according to the Brisbane *Topic*, he was "one of the wealthiest actors in England"—with a fortune of between a quarter and half a million pounds.

In the 1940s, with their emphasis on bravery, on practicality and external survival, Olivier with his unselfconscious earthiness and sense of excitement had as an actor reigned supreme. "He had a very secure poetic sense of history," John Osborne said in a 1973 tribute. "Like Churchill in a sense. When he went in to bat he felt he was batting for England. He wasn't simply an actor, he did have this sense of belonging to history."

Vivien Leigh, generally thought to be the most beautiful actress of her day, had made her name in the film roles of Scarlett O'Hara, Myra in *Waterloo Bridge*, Lady Hamilton, Cleopatra in Shaw's *Caesar and Cleopatra*, Anna Karenina and, in her best stage performance up to this time, Sabina in Thornton Wilder's *The Skin of Our Teeth*. With her wit and enormous concentration—and combining many differing shades of ambition with a driving egotism—she personified stardom: above all she had, as Edith Evans described it, the "primitive passport" of her looks. It let her in everywhere.

The extra dimension shared by both consisted of their passion. Since their cloak-and-dagger first meetings in 1935, the liaison they conducted quickly became a celebrated love story, not losing its appeal after their marriage in August 1940.* Though as a story it incorporated a strong manufactured element—Alexander Korda, for instance, exploited its publicity value quite shamelessly in *Lady Hamilton* (1941) —the story itself never stopped fascinating the public. Its appeal grew even stronger when Olivier was knighted in July

* In his autobiography Olivier records the date as 21 August: actually it was 31 August.

1947. It was as if the now Sir Laurence and Lady Olivier, still with the looks to create an image of idealised eroticism, had been elevated into the select company of mythologised lovers. Although the end of the war had brought with it widespread disillusionment with heroism and with the romantic self-sacrifice that so-called pure love might entail, their hold over the popular imagination still increased. Their apparent great love for one another would not have had such appeal had it not shown—as if both chose by "instinct" or "fate" a way of life in which life imitated art—most of the conditions and many circumstances of a fictional love story. For example, had Vivien been a character in Tolstoy she could not have done better than to marry as she did, when young, pretty, and undecided in character, the decent and civilised barrister, Leigh Holman, who could provide security and good sense from which she then needed escape into the fulfilment of "dark" passion. Probably neither she nor Olivier, himself married to a loyal and compared to him relatively mature partner, the actress Jill Esmond—who also provided him with a stable relationship—would have been attracted to the other, had both been unmarried and available. But both found themselves at the stage where they needed to tap greater resources of feeling.

They met, then, in circumstances already highly charged with emotion where the interplay of guilt, the dramatic claims of "passion", the obstacles placed in the way of their fulfilling their love by the respective partners served to intensify further what seemed to both of them a pure commitment. Passion, in their case, appeared largely unconnected with sex. So both, while behaving in terms which in the mid-1930s were scandalous, never entirely forfeited public sympathy, and exalted, by the mythological quality they gave to it, the fashion and practice of adultery.

Although portrayed in most literature and drama as a misfortune, passionate love in real life goes largely unrecognised as such. When Vivien Leigh visited Olivier backstage after he played Romeo in John Gielgud's production of *Romeo and Juliet* (1935) at the Old Vic and implanted on his shoulder a soft little kiss, she said—or so it was reported—that she would, whatever the cost, capture him. James Agate described in the *Sunday Times* the pull of Olivier's Romeo:

> Apart from the speaking, there was poetry to spare. This Romeo looked every inch a lover and a lover fey and foredoomed. The actor's facial expression was varied and mobile, his bearing noble, his play of arm imaginative, and his smaller gestures were infinitely touching. Note, for example, how lovingly he fingered first the props of Juliet's balcony and at the last her bier. For once in a way the tide of this young man's passion was presented at the flood, and his grief was agonisingly done.

Her background more than prepared Vivien in her response to such an image. The facts of her life are that she was born Vivian Mary Hartley in Darjeeling, India, on 5 November 1913. Her early upbringing had combined, in explosive measures, unreality, mystery, loyalty, treachery, as well as discipline, good taste and virtuous aspiration. She had travelled widely, been educated in Catholic convents in England, France, Italy and Switzerland. Her mother was a staunch Catholic of Irish-French descent, her father a genial horse-breeder with a love of theatre and a taste for ladies: his secret life clearly appealed to his only child in her most formative years.

Shortly after Vivien's marriage in December 1932 to Leigh Holman (she took his christian name as her stage surname), she was presented at Court to King George V and Queen Mary, and enacted the ceremony as if in a dream. When her first and only child, Suzanne Holman, was born ten months after the marriage Vivien immediately passed her over to the care of a nanny. On later occasions she would sometimes not even remember the date of her birthday. Her marriage to Holman, shielding and nurturing as it did her aspiration of becoming an actress, had been no less eventful than her subsequent attraction to Olivier. Holman quickly found himself manoeuvred into the position of giving his wife freedom to pursue her independent life before realising he should never have done so. Vivien's wilfulness in this respect could perhaps never have remained wholly checked, though she did apparently love Holman and even when he eventually divorced her she remained on affectionate terms with him, still needing the stability of his friendship and understanding.

But as she had been drawn into the quickening tempo of a successful career so too had Vivien seemed to need more and more a "deep" and "real" love, and between the time when she and Olivier first became entangled, and the time five years later when they married it becomes hard to distinguish fact and imaginative embellishment—except that clearly it was she who forced the pace, she whose intensity and need for excitement acted as catalyst to the break-up of Olivier's marriage to Jill Esmond.

While Jill Esmond was pregnant with Olivier's first child, and while on the surface Vivien behaved in a friendly way towards Jill, Vivien and Olivier would arrange their secret, though outwardly chaste, trysts. A friend, Oswald Frewen, reported:

> Larry worked with Viv almost every day. He'd go up to her house in Shepherd Market in the mornings and they'd work on her voice and line delivery. Then, often, they'd go out to lunch. Leigh knew all about it but he didn't pay it any attention. He assumed it was just another of those theatrical relationships. Jill Esmond knew about it too. She was fat with child by then, which I suppose made Vivien that much more attractive to Larry. But I don't think Jill ever had a whisper of an idea that Larry had more on his mind than helping out a young actress friend to both of them.

This outward-seeming chasteness grew to be a measure of their devotion to the art of acting. This code of behaviour must have made both think that they could ignore ordinary morality, but Vivien, by breaking their previous ties and binding Olivier to her, became the dominant partner. There were instances of Olivier wavering, returning to Jill and his young son Tarquin, of him expressing doubt and guilt over Vivien to his friends. Tyrone Guthrie, who asked Olivier and Vivien to play Hamlet and Ophelia at Elsinore, allowing the lovers to flee from their respective spouses into a Liebestod setting where strains of Wagner could almost be heard in the waves dashing against the ancient ramparts, aptly summed up, in an interview in 1971, Olivier's mood:

> For a young man who had everything going for him in his career, Larry was profoundly unhappy at the time. It all had to do with the conflict between his violent and immature love for Vivien . . . and his more mature, subdued attachment to Jill . . . He was literally in a quandary as to what to do. When I first talked to him about *Hamlet*, he said, "Oh no, how I'd love to do it, I already know what it feels like to be a Hamlet in real life" . . . He believed he had a great deal of personal Hamlet-like anguish and spiritual paralysis to bring to the part.

Instinctively Olivier knew that the way for him to develop as an actor was to be found through his relationship with Vivien. This choice may not have been wholly conscious, but the unconscious drive of his personality must have been towards such a mixture of the real and the unreal as Vivien embodied. His own mother had, when he was twelve, died of a brain tumour. She had been, as he said, "lovely—there is no photograph that I have seen which has revealed this in anything like its true measure". Many years later he told Kenneth Tynan that upon her death he felt such desolation that he thought of going down to Chelsea Bridge and jumping off. She became a fantasy figure to him and her loss may help to explain that curious amoral strength and cold inner quality on which many have remarked.

Awareness of death, connected with deep love and a sense of bereavement, was a strong factor in Olivier's early development, and he formed no compensatory closeness with his clergyman father, towards whom he concealed resentment mixed with awe and a sense of his unapproachability. As a very young man he was always falling passionately in love but this hunger caused by the loss of his mother remained only partially satisfied for a long time. He had, by his own admission, a coquettish side to his character ("in psychological terms, I suppose, it is a feminine trait of the worst kind"), which with Jill Esmond almost ruined his chances.

His inclination, already, was to dramatise relationships and indulge in fantasies about them. Soon after his first marriage, as he later said, his dreams of high sexuality were not to be realised, "which was depressing and soon became oppressive". But he subdued his personal unhappiness in tireless dedication to work. And when he first set eyes on what he called "this wondrous unimagined beauty" of Vivien's in Ashley Dukes's *The Mask of Virtue* (1935) he became moved almost to lyrical rapture; her neck, "almost too fragile to support her head", gave her an unexpected quality of surprise, something "of the pride of the master juggler who can make a brilliant manoeuvre appear almost accidental". The attraction, he noted in his autobiography, was "of the most perturbing nature I had ever encountered".

Danger, suspense, drama, shock. With his impressionable and volatile nature—in him fortunately linked to more stable qualities—his feelings too rapidly became more "real" than anything else, or, in other words, stronger than anything else in the emotional demand they made on him. He therefore gives the impression that he and Vivien were not brought together in any ordinary way.

In a romantic novel, or other work of fiction, a reader condones liberties the author takes to keep the passion simmering. The same kind of tacit consent and encouragement surrounded Olivier and Vivien in the initial stages of their passion. Alexander Korda, being personally attracted by both of them but knowing also that in terms of film-making he had found in them the perfect dream couple, helped them—in particular during the filming of *Fire over England* and *Twenty-one Days* in 1936–7—as if taking a personal hand in administering the love potion. But above all, from the force of their unfinished personalities, they created a sense of inevitability about their ultimate union.

Up until the time that he met Vivien, Olivier, both as an actor and a man, had been a magpie with thievish habits, a personality amalgam of the best bits of his friends and those he admired, as well as of the characters he had played. He was the supreme impersonator, but there had been no centre, either on stage or off, to his impersonations. His main assets were his athletic ability and his good looks. His first teacher, Elsie

Fogerty, when she met him as an aspiring acting student, had at once penetrated his weakness. He noticed, he recalled, her shading her eyes top and bottom so as to isolate part of his face. She placed "the tip of her little finger on my forehead against the base of my remarkably low hair-line, and slid it down to rest in the deep hollow of my brow-line and the top of my nose". "You have weakness . . . here," she pronounced.

Olivier—his precocious self-perception foreshadowing later achievements as self-editor of performances on stage and on film—was at once aware of the truth she had spoken, but could do nothing about it until he discovered, as he put it in his autobiography,

> the protective shelter of nose-putty and enjoyed a pleasurable sense of relief and relaxation when some character part called for a sculptural addition to my face, affording the shelter of an alien character and enabling me to avoid anything so embarrassing as self-representation.

Olivier's involvement with Vivien stimulated a sudden transformation of personality; he became more outgoing and more able than before to respond to challenges. She took him to the very limit of his capacity for love, which mobilised, as never before, his talent. Vivien appeared wise. Vivien had command. "She could have been Prime Minister," said Wilfred Hyde-White, "for nothing ever deterred her from getting her way." She was particularly suited to the role of muse and oracle. She inspired in men over whom she cast a spell intoxication rather than sexual passion. "In the days of matriarchy," wrote the critic Alan Dent, "she would have been one of those Cretan goddess-priestesses, capable of making men great and equally capable of destroying them." Dent emphasised her potential danger—both to herself and others.

After the initial pain caused to their respective partners, after the surges of guilt and destructive feeling—and their own torments of separation and uncertainty—Vivien's influence over Olivier became beneficial, and added a heroic dimension to what he did. It was, as he later acknowledged (though not in his autobiography), her driving ambition and her belief in him that sustained and carried him along with her; she broke down

his innate shyness and reserve with strangers outside the
theatre circle, and as a hostess helped him entertain; she also
educated his tastes.

The film of *Henry V*, a colossal feat of co-ordination and
self-confidence, was the most striking example of her beneficial effect. In his first seasons at the Old Vic, daring at last to
come out of his shell or, rather, to cast off the nose putty that
was often the psychological crux of his impersonation, Olivier
had found his identity as an actor. As he observed of what
others saw as his shattering performance in Sophocles'
Oedipus, "I didn't dare to expose myself until I had played
Oedipus" (and even for this he kept a little putty). The risks
undergone with Vivien, the torments shared, the suffering
received with knowledge as its compensatory gift had, in a
sense, paid off. But the advance brought with it its own danger.

It was the director Tyrone Guthrie who first gave Olivier
the key to what had been holding him back as an actor. With
the Old Vic Company in Shaw's *Arms and the Man*, Olivier had
been acting Sergius and had, when they opened in Manchester
in August 1944 (prior to the opening of *Peer Gynt* in London),
received—in contrast to Ralph Richardson as Bluntschli—a
bad notice in the *Manchester Guardian*. This made him very
disconsolate, so that when Guthrie visited him on the second
night Guthrie asked, on receiving the glum response to his
congratulations, "Why don't you like the part?" Olivier
looked at him incredulously, "What?" Guthrie looked back at
him: "Don't you love Sergius?" Olivier had expostulated,
"Love that stooge? That inconsiderable . . . God, Tony, if you
weren't so tall I'd hit you, if I could reach you."

Olivier reported, probably unfairly, that up to then Guthrie
had never given him much enlightening general advice but had
always stuck to technicalities. But that night he told him
something that changed the course of his actor's thinking for
the rest of his life. "Well, of course, if you can't love him you'll
never be any good in him, will you?"

It took Olivier the inside of a week to get used to the idea; by
the end of it he loved Sergius as he had never loved anybody.
"I loved him for his faults, for his showing off, his absurdity,
his bland doltishness. Vivien came up for the Saturday night
and was ecstatic about it—probably all the more so because

from what I had said she had learnt to expect the worst."

At another time he recounted the turning point with Guthrie in the form that one can never be successful unless one gets right inside the character and learns to love him as one loves oneself. But, however he proposed or explained to himself this significant change, there is little doubt that, from the time of its discovery, his acting became totally transformed. At the same time this coincided with his technical maturity. All through his life, it would seem, the capacity for love had not found its full expression. He could never love his mother enough because she had died when he was still only a boy; his first marriage to Jill Esmond had denied his overwhelming need to love both its sexual and emotional outlet (he is cruelly candid about this in his autobiography). Vivien he truly loved—she represented an ideal, undoubtedly, but the years of their illicit relationship, and now of their marriage, had not resulted in any satisfactory expression of love. At first it had been all external obstacles—their married partners conspiring to keep them apart, the trials of separation, war —and now there was a secondary line of obstacles building up: the obstacles within.

The striking thing about Olivier's next large role after Sergius, Shakespeare's Richard III, was the degree to which Olivier loved and totally identified with the evil in the man, and therefore brought out all his comic and grotesque colouring. He found at first when he came to doubling Hotspur and Justice Shallow to Ralph Richardson's Falstaff in the Old Vic production of the two parts of *Henry IV*, that to switch from loving one role to loving another in so short a time was extremely difficult, but this too eased in the face of his determination. Loving two characters at the same time, he attested, was as tricky as loving two women at the same time—but then he found the answer. "I realised that the reason you fall in love with one woman is because you are no longer able to love the woman who came before and yet you still have all this love in you." That understood he would, when he had finished with Shallow, put him out of his mind, force himself not to love Shallow, then turn all his love, like some powerful beam of energy, on to Harry Hotspur. Hotspur would then be dismissed in favour of Shallow again. A stupendously danger-

ous trick of self-manipulation had been learned, more dangerous than the spectacular athletic feats he liked to perform.

Vivien might be forgiven for sometimes wondering which he
now loved the more, his acting or herself. Ambitious though
she was, her artistry lacked profoundness just because,
perhaps, she still put so much energy into living and her acting
remained largely an extension of her personality. Olivier
returned the attention she gave him in the Svengali-like power
he held over her career, moulding her appearance and talent as
he did his own. But for all the simplicity of her feeling for
Olivier, her interplay of motive and temperament was more
complex.

In September 1942, after Vivien had miscarried, Alan Dent,
who later edited the texts for the films of *Henry V* and *Hamlet*,
recalled the "fragile beauty of Viv waving goodbye along the
corridor outside a private suite in Claridge's". She had been
"wearing an invalid's shawl of the purest, whitest and softest
wool". Despite the miscarriage she and Dent had just dined
well: on croquettes de fruits de mer, on roast partridge with
fresh green haricots and salad, washed down with two different burgundies—so perhaps one ought not to be too sorry for
her, especially in late 1942. As long as she could get away with
it she made the minimum concessions to ill-health.

Just after the European war finished in May 1945, and after
her first performance as Sabina in *The Skin of Our Teeth* at the
Phoenix Theatre, she had suffered her first major collapse.
Never, since childhood, had she slept much at night. She had
always been burdened with coughs and colds. In early 1945 she
and Olivier had bought Notley Abbey, an old stone abbey in
Buckinghamshire, where she took charge of restoring and
refurbishing the interior, while Olivier left with the Old Vic
ENSA tour of the newly liberated territories of Europe. At
Notley, from a mixture of strain and excitement, she grew
excessively tired. Her now persistent cough worsened, and
was accompanied by recurrent fever. She also began showing
the alarming symptoms of an unhappy mental condition, such
as heavy drinking or outbursts of violent temper, of which she
herself, in her normal state, seemed unaware.

The tendency towards illness reflected an inner uncertainty. As a child a profound Catholic sense of guilt had been instilled in her by her mother and by her devout Catholic upbringing, and she still felt deeply unhappy over the wrong she had done Leigh Holman and their daughter, looking to Olivier's love to reassure her and make her forget this guilt. In contrast, a wilful side to her character almost enjoyed self-destruction and relished abusing the high expectation of parents and others as she perversely pushed herself to her physical and emotional limits. But this proclivity was concealed by her English upper-class manner which made disease seem morally neutral.

Even diagnosis of tuberculosis in one lung did not deter her from continuing to perform in *The Skin of Our Teeth*. She had received excellent notices for it. Sabina was a part which exactly suited her limited stage abilities. "Her natural voice had a practical, sensible, slightly amused tone which went well in comedy," wrote Alan Dent. Other critics found her mannered and too precise, and censured every effect, night after night, for being exactly the same. Would she ever become a tragic actress, they would ask, for when it came to tragedy she always had to assume a voice. Yet she herself had excellent critical judgment. Olivier always valued her for it. Her teasing pronouncements amused everybody, and she, like Olivier, had a marvellous eye for detail.

In 1945, at the end of July, she was forced to retire from *The Skin of Our Teeth*, and Olivier, who by then had returned from the Old Vic tour in Europe, took her into hospital, and then to convalesce at Notley where she remained in bed for much of the winter. In the meantime Olivier himself, in a wig of virile dark curls and with sharp and trenchant nose, had, as Oedipus, been imitating the ermine's agony in his climactic blood-curdling scream. Vivien's reduction by the action of illness to total passivity, making her when she grew well again much less ethereal—she had grown quite plump—reinforced her determination to live even more fiercely. By the following summer, when she accompanied Olivier with the Old Vic tour to New York, she had almost completely recovered, although she had not got over the tension caused by inactivity. "A crazy quarrel last night with Vivien," reported the playwright Garson Kanin in a diary entry for May 1946. (It was over the pronunciation of the title of Machiavelli's play *Mandragola*.) "It must be maddening for her, a young actress at the peak of her powers and popularity, to find herself in the position of a hanger-on who has come along for the ride."

But to portray already by 1945—as several other biographers have done—Vivien as victim and Olivier as survivor, is anachronistic. She may have had a sense that Olivier did more than she, but she had not fallen into hysterical depression or sexual excess, nor had Olivier, as one biographer wrote, become anxious that "Vivien, like some exquisite fragile piece of porcelain, would crack and disintegrate". When it came to Olivier's film of *Hamlet* she, being highly self-critical, must have known that she was too old to play Ophelia (the part went to Jean Simmons). Both she and Olivier were a lot more solid and impassive, more thick-skinned and resilient—and as working actress and actor more mindful and conserving of their energies—than is generally depicted. Together they had a peculiar hardness and awareness—even a conspiratorial closeness about the eminence they shared; like precocious children who have everything, they were also terrifyingly innocent of some quite ordinary things. But in the fall of 1946, some months after the trip to New York, when Olivier had again departed for the continent—this time with the Old Vic production of *King Lear*—and when he was also preparing the film of *Hamlet*, Vivien's mood worsened. The consolation of Korda's offer, in 1947, of *Anna Karenina* should have reestablished her as a film star, but the script was inferior and Julien Duvivier's direction lacked any kind of inspiration. The role also forced her back on herself, and without Olivier, who should have been cast as Vronsky and who could then have made her project her feelings outwards, she found it painful and humiliating.* Anna's life, as recounted by Tolstoy, was an extremely moral story which—with strong similarities to the Tristan and Iseult love story—equates the pursuit of passionate love and adultery with death. By having to relive so much

---

* "Wasn't it dangerous to marry an actress?" a *New York Times* interviewer asked Olivier in 1979. He replied, "As long as the man is master it works. It begins to fail when the woman becomes a rival and wants to master the man."

that was close to her own first marriage with Leigh Holman, Vivien's feelings of guilt were revived.

Cecil Beaton noticed the dramatic change that had overtaken her when, one morning in July 1947, he called on her in her dressing room. The newspapers had just announced Olivier's knighthood, and Beaton expected to find her in a great state of elation:

> I open the door. "Oh, I'm so happy for you about the great news!" A face of fury is reflected in the mirror. "Really it's too stupid. Would you believe it—the dressmaker from Paris was waiting at her hotel the entire day yesterday and the studio forgot to order a car for her. Really—I've never worked on such a film as this!"

By the completion of *Hamlet* in November 1947 she had become fearful that, like Anna in that profoundly depressing section of the book near the end when she suspects Vronsky no longer loves her, there was a limit being set to the length of her own and Olivier's love, which on the Antipodean tour, would now, as never before, be tested against the reality of the people they were. For after long periods when they had been, for the greater part of the time, separated, they now had a whole year in which they would be, day and night, together.

2   On the High Seas

"Unpacked for the night," ran Olivier's diary entry for his first evening on board the SS *Corinthic*, "dinner alone together in cabin. Vivien not eating much. Went for a walk by myself wearing duffel coat. Poured bath, but went to bed without it. Read Logan Pearsall Smith's *English Aphorisms* for a while before turning out the light."

The *Corinthic*, a 15,000-ton refrigerated cargo ship of the Shaw-Savill line, carried also one hundred first-class passengers, nearly forty of them from the Old Vic Company. In charge was the benign, white-haired Captain Robertson, known as "Robbie". "He really is a most charming man, kindly, with a great understanding and tolerance of youth and the youngsters adore him," wrote Elsie Beyer, the Company's General Manager, a middle-aged woman who wore trim suits of tweed, and who had very recently left the offices of H. M. Tennent, the theatrical producers, in order to manage the tour. Previous to this she had been a Sister at Westminster Hospital and a secretary to Wolf Barnato, the racing driver. "Captain Robertson generally spent a number of hours with them on deck at night, answering all and sundry questions and thoroughly entering into the spirit of their fun." She added, concealing she might have a specific personal interest in him: "The Purser, Mr Oliver, is also the most charming man." Mr Oliver was the son of the captain of the *Titanic*; the shadow of that appalling disaster, it was said, had remained bottled up inside him.

From the start of the month-long outward journey romance undoubtedly was in the air—but also acute homesickness. Eileen Beldon, forty-seven years of age and the second female lead (after Vivien), had left behind a twelve-year-old son and a husband who was an RAF pilot. For the first few days she wept and wept in her cabin, never even appearing at breakfast. She had been cast in the parts that Athene Seyler had first been approached to play, but Olivier had not wanted Nicholas Hannen, Athene Seyler's husband, to accompany them (he considered Hannen, who played Buckingham in the original 1944 production of *Richard III*, a bit passé) and had felt he could not ask her without including him.

Peter Cushing had better fortune with his spouse. His first job with Olivier had been as Osric on the film of *Hamlet*, during which, through abscess poisoning, he lost three of his front teeth. Olivier told him, to help him over the embarrassment of wearing a plate, "You are afraid of spitting at people . . . [He put his face a few inches from Cushing's] Drown me: it will be a glorious death—so long as we can hear what you are saying." On being asked to join the tour, Cushing told Olivier the only thing that bothered him was the thought of being parted from his wife. "I'll have none of that," Olivier replied. "There was too much of it forced upon most of us during the war. You bring Helen [Beck] with you." So he did. Of Polish émigré parents, and formerly a dancer, she played small parts and helped backstage.

The voyage came after eight years of war and stringent restrictions. The *Corinthic* stopped off first at Las Palmas where the Company spent the day ashore sightseeing, slaking their thirsts with iced white wine and haggling over big straw hats and other souvenirs.

The Oliviers' closest friends in the Company were George Relph and his Sydney-born wife Mercia Swinburne. Born in 1886, Relph had acted juvenile leads before World War I and played with both Sir Herbert Beerbohm Tree and Sir Frank Benson. He had been disfigured by war injury and a later motor accident, and his career did not regain its former momentum until, near the end of the 1930s, he re-emerged as a rich character actor, wonderfully smooth in the Gerald du Maurier style. Later he joined the New Theatre seasons when he played Gloucester in *King Lear* and a brilliant Subtle to Ralph Richardson's Face in Ben Jonson's *The Alchemist*. He had met his wife on a previous tour in Australia—he had acted Shakespeare there many years before with Oscar Asche and Lily Brayton. But few other members of the Company had much experience of foreign travel. Some, such as a young married couple, Georgina Jumel, a touchingly pretty girl with light brown hair, and Terence Morgan, had never travelled abroad. The Morgans had had to leave their eight-month-old daughter, Lyvia-Lee (named after Olivier and Leigh), behind in England.

After only a few days at sea, and in spite of his intention to make the first week a complete rest, Olivier asked the Purser to arrange rehearsal space. They toured the ship and settled on the dining-room. But when he first tried out Sir Peter Teazle (in *The School for Scandal*, due as their opening play in Australia), Olivier felt a "burning pain like white hot needles in right toe getting v. bad. Went to see Doctor afterwards. He said it was not gout [in fact it was]. He said rest it, so I played deck quoits." He went to bed, slept well, and next day anointed and soaked the foot—and got one of the actors to hear him as Teazle. The same evening they dined at the captain's table: "Vivien turned to me suddenly with an alarmingly wild look and said: 'Tonight I should like to play dominoes'."

Olivier had, as much as was possible, chosen married couples to form the nucleus of the Company. Besides the Relphs, the Morgans, the Cushings, and himself and Vivien, he had engaged, in addition to Eileen Beldon whose husband was still flying, four single women: Anne McGrath, Meg Maxwell, Peggy Simpson (these three known as the "ladies-in-waiting" on Vivien, with Mercia Swinburne "chief lady-in-waiting") and Jane Shirley, the daughter of Angela Baddeley, who as well as acting in small parts also helped backstage. Single men outnumbered the women two to one: most noticeable of these were the blond-haired Dan Cunningham and dark-haired Thomas Heathcote, and the older character actor Bernard Merefield. The others, in addition to the three who had gone ahead, were James Bailey, Robert Beaumont, George Cooper, Tony Gavin, Oliver Hunter, Derrick Penley and Hugh Stewart. Dan Cunningham had the looks of a juvenile male lead: cast as Richmond, he had, at the end of *Richard III*, the job of fighting with Olivier.

When in late 1946 plans for the tour were mooted *Richard III*, which had already toured in Europe in 1945, had been picked unanimously for the Olivier performance that most Australians and New Zealanders wanted to see. To balance it the revival of a modern play, Thornton Wilder's *The Skin of Our Teeth*, would, the Old Vic Governors hoped, tap the drawing power of Vivien's name—at this time greater than Olivier's. Whatever the merits of the play she could, as she had already successfully shown, impose her own vitality on it. Yet the Governors of the Old Vic and the British Council criticised it for being, instead of British, an American folk play, although Olivier, being on excellent terms with the Chairman of the Governors, Lord Lytton, overrode their criticism and had his own way.

Olivier's choice of Sheridan's *The School for Scandal* was adventurous and unopposed. Determined to widen his experience as a director he knew *School* would give him the opportunity to do so, also providing equal roles for both Vivien and himself, and a wide range of solid parts for the rest of the Company. To show his love of the play he quoted Beerbohm Tree: "Few will dispute that *The School for Scandal* is the most brilliant comedy that has been given to the world."

On the sixth day out they began rehearsing seriously, although the boat was "rolling about in a mocking way which made the prancing even less graceful than usual". In bed Vivien, far from playing dominoes, read out to Olivier occasional passages from *More Trivia*:

> I look at my overcoat and my hat hanging in the hall with reassurance, for although I go out of doors with one individuality today, when yesterday I had quite another, yet my clothes keep various selves buttoned up together, and enable all those otherwise aggregates of psychological phenomena to pass themselves off as one person.

On the seventh day Olivier found himself bogged down with the Sheridan: "Where it is human it comes instantly alive and presents no difficulty, where it is artificial it seems hearsed in death unable to burst its cerements, and, to prevent the audience dying as stiff as our ancestors in 1780, has to have arbitrary choreography thrust upon it."

Drawn to the realistic side of the play, Olivier would have preferred solid scenery, but because the sets had to travel all through Australia and New Zealand Cecil Beaton had designed them in the style of eighteenth-century engravings, using trompe l'oeil, and had even introduced hatching strokes into the costumes.

The Company carried all the costumes on board, and on the eighth day Mrs Jacobs, one of the wardrobe staff who had been indisposed, missing a previous inspection, discovered a trunk had been broken into and some costumes taken. Wireless instructions to obtain replacements were issued. Rehearsals now took place daily, usually in the morning, and for the rest of the time they played deck tennis, housey-housey and swam in a canvas pool rigged up near the mast. Most of the Company had cabins with windows looking over the top deck. In the evening they would play "The Game", the prototype of modern television's *Give Us a Clue* and referred to on another occasion by Cecil Beaton as "an elaborate form of dumb crambo"—which grew so popular that the non-theatrical passengers used to gather as an audience.

On the thirteenth day the sun shone directly overhead. The actor Tony Gavin commented to Olivier, "The worst of it is that all our tooth-glasses taste of Gin and Andrews' [liver salts]." When rehearsals dragged they watched flying fish and hammerhead sharks: no improvement, Olivier commented, on his and Vivien's, as Lady Teazle, second quarrel: "but some beautiful porpoises and another shark cheered things up".

Olivier need not have worried for all three plays were in good shape. They had already rehearsed for over two months in Donald Wolfit's scenery repository near the women's prison in Holloway. Being very damp this had not been all that comfortable, prompting George Relph's comment, "This place is damp with the tears of actors who never got paid." Vivien coughed a lot. For these rehearsals they had not been paid either, but on the outward trip they received half salary, which amounted, in the case of Terence Morgan and Georgina Jumel, to £15 and £6 respectively. To provide incidental music the Company included two members of the Musicians' Union who were already on full pay, and apart from Olivier and Vivien, the musicians, claimed the actors later, earned more on the tour than anyone else. But it did not excite much envy. English actors, in contrast to their Australian counterparts, were prepared to rehearse long hours for nothing. Some rejoiced in being driven hard: "Politics has destroyed the theatre," Eileen Beldon said; "in rehearsal it is often only at the point of exhaustion when you vanish and the part is there."

On board Vivien had plenty of spare time. She and Olivier had chosen a sea passage rather than flying because, eighteen months before, both had barely escaped death on a Pan

American Constellation which had caught fire over Connecticut. One of its engines had fallen off and the pilot made a brilliant forced landing. Also, Olivier hoped, the sea air and the rest would improve Vivien's health. So she would sit in a deck chair wrapped in coats and blankets, wearing sunglasses, surrounded by some of the younger men, and drinking black velvet (champagne and Guinness).

She had lost none of her exquisite beauty: the piercing blue-green eyes; the delightful turned-up nose now freckling in the tropical light; the softly moulded brow with its border of tiny dark hairs springing back from the hairline, the beginnings of glorious curls—all these and more reflected, or suggested, a passionate and vulnerable nature and its delicate balance between emotion and intellect, between fantasy and the real.

Yet she was a strange woman. Her thoughts more often than not were a curious jumble. Sometimes, as she told risqué stories in the way a man would tell them, listeners would wonder how deep her femininity went, and whether she was not a man masquerading in slim and fragile loveliness. To those who saw Olivier and her together her personality seemed complctcly to smother his. Yet though she had quick perception and a close memory of the detail of her friends' lives—even, in order to avoid repetition, keeping a book to jot down menus she gave dinner guests—her mind lacked method. All her life she had been terribly spoiled; "God and the Angel" was how some of the Company, adopting a fashion dating from the early Korda films, had already dubbed Olivier and her.

Trivial things brought her pleasure: clothes—she enjoyed being a front-page beauty; her Siamese cat, New (named after the theatre), whom she had left behind in Durham Cottage, and to whom, indulging a child-like fantasy, she now began to write letters, signing herself "Clara the alley cat". (Indeed Olivier's nickname for Vivien was "Puss".) But she thought rarely of children: like many theatrical stars she treated herself with the care and indulgence with which one might treat a child and to her, as to them, a real child was a threat. Her delight in the externals of existence had its reflection in the wardrobe she had on board: fourteen evening gowns, fourteen afternoon dresses and ten suits and a large number of hats, shoes and carefully chosen accessories.

At the end of February the *Corinthic* anchored off Cape Town and the Company made their second trip ashore. Olivier and Vivien had their first taste of being treated like royalty: (from the diary) "Docked by five o'clock, came below and changed for dreaded Press party. Flowers, fruit, messages and mail in profusion came flying into the cabin." The Shaw-Savill line gave a cocktail party which was followed by a visit to see Ivor Novello in *Perchance to Dream*; the following day a fleet of cars took them touring, afterwards dropping them off at another cocktail party at High Commission House ("Twelve-and-a-half per cent, I suppose," quipped Vivien).

On 3 March, in brilliant sunshine, they set sail out of Table Bay to Fremantle. But soon the *Corinthic* met the infamous Cape Rollers. Elsie Beyer observed that if any theatrical management wanted to calm down a company they should put them on the sea between Cape Town and Fremantle. The temperature grew cold, the ship heaved and rolled, the wind howled terribly. Later the sea got calmer, and on the final and more peaceful part of the Indian Ocean crossing albatrosses accompanied them.

About 5 am on 14 March they arrived off Fremantle, steaming slowly up river as they picked up the pilot, the immigration officer and the doctor. On the same launch a dozen press and film people appeared and these had to be locked in the purser's room until the passengers had been cleared by the doctor. Olivier himself "Woke at seven, feeling worse than I remember since [my] first evening of Irish whiskey with Roger [Furse] and Dallas [Bower] in Dublin 1943 . . . Vivien quite all right. Press on board, interviews, flashbulbs, newsreels, and a broadcast before we knew what we were doing."

In those days aboard each new ship that reached harbour the banks would send a representative to attend to the finances of passengers. So a motley crowd of bankers, press men and British Council representatives met them at 8 am when they finally docked. "Last night when we were fifty miles out to sea we smelt gum tips," began Olivier's greeting. "We know practically nothing about Australia. We want to see the country. We want to see every kind of animal or bird there is. Black swans, for instance; why aren't there any here?"—he said this looking around the crowd on the quayside. "Where are they, anyway?"

"What *is* a billabong?" piped up Vivien, who had pinned to her lapel a large corsage of frangipani given by a well-wisher. The temperature had passed 100 degrees and was climbing by the minute. In spite of this she told the crowd that they had been learning "Waltzing Matilda" in which the word "billabong" occurred. Someone explained that a billabong was a deserted river course where the stream has been flowing in a meander and had cut across its neck, leaving a river lake in the former course of the river. She took it all in. Her deep, blue-green eyes glittered as she recounted how hard they had been rehearsing on the *Corinthic* and how, playing at deck quoits, she had broken two finger-nails.

The reporters noted that Lady Olivier—not much over five feet tall—had a slight figure with a tiny nipped-in waist which the padded hip-line of her suit emphasised. The suit, of brown wool with a light fleck, could be classed as in the latest Parisian style, while the pleated skirt ended exactly twelve inches from the ground. An emerald green snood, pinned at the back by two jewelled hat pins, framed her face. Her walking shoes were casuals of brown and white, and she carried a large, initialled handbag. The triple strand of pearls did not escape notice, nor did the earrings of gold leaf design, set with emeralds: these—with the cluster of rubies and diamonds on her fingers—made a dazzling effect.

"My first plan is to buy a suit," Olivier, still dressed in winter grey, glumly observed. "The lightest I can find." The day before the weather had been dull and chilly. They had been told that in March, which was the end of the summer in Australia, heatwaves were rare. In the blinding glare both he and Vivien put on a brave face, smiled and chatted vivaciously and, almost at once, found themselves a hit with the crowd.

3 Perth

In the end the people of Perth had responded warmly to the appeal for accommodation. The flat (16 Bellevue) made available to the Oliviers was superbly placed on a hill looking east over the Swan River and west over King's Park. Perth itself they found pretty, though not much of a city. Cynthia Nolan, the travel writer and wife of the painter Sidney Nolan, described it at this time as

> Grimy, dishevelled, noisy . . . an overgrown country town which has lost its fresh charm without yet having developed any compensating dignity or culture although the city fathers have had the presight to reserve large areas of natural bush along the waterfront . . . make illegal the picking of wild flowers and erect, amid trees and gardens, a free university of somewhat contemporary design.

Visiting their flat, Viv was struck at once with the view over the yacht-filled Swan: she rushed to the French windows, flung them open, but then looked highly disappointed: "What, no koalas?" The only thing remotely approaching koalas seen that day had been the ten members of the Company's advance party, now reunited with the others, and who since their arrival a week earlier had been roasting on the beaches to dark brown or red colour—and feeding largely on melon and ice cream.

Having approved the flat, which caught the evening breeze and seemed very private (they did not know the lady owner had told all her friends), the Oliviers, accompanied by the Relphs and Eileen Beldon, lunched at the Esplanade Hotel with the British Council representatives, and with the impresario and on-the-spot organiser of the tour, Dan O'Connor, owner of a steel mill in Auckland, New Zealand.

They at once warmed to O'Connor: retiring in manner and known as "the man with the sack of gold", he had a sense of humour and an ability to smooth the path ahead. Passionate about Shakespeare, he professed his two strongest dislikes to be income tax and the unions.

After lunch a visit to the Capitol Theatre, where they were

due to play, dampened their hopes: looking at the great barn-like interior which seated 2,280 people—it had been used as concert hall, cinema, and Variety, or "legit", theatre— Olivier declared, "We'd better dress up as Christians and throw ourselves to the lions!" Backstage facilities were poor, with only two small changing rooms, the largest of which the management insisted Olivier and Vivien take.

This visit over, they went down to Scarborough Beach "for a wonderful drive as the sun went down", wrote Olivier. "A black swan flew over us afterwards. If I don't sleep tonight I never will."

That night the Company variously settled in all over Perth. Most of the younger members, having grown up during the war, had never seen such food as they were served during the day: succulent lamb chops; huge steaks with eggs on them; oysters; fresh milk and butter; lashings of beer—the profusion almost made them weep. Not surprisingly, they ate as much as they could and felt very uncomfortable.

In a suburb twenty-year-old Michael Redington tasted the novel delights of an open-air cinema, watching Frank Sinatra: "One watches the film, then sleeps a bit, then watches the film again." The Oliviers lay together in their flat with its cool evening breeze: "Strange birds jabber and laugh and squawk at us in various hitherto unknown ways," said Olivier. The women—most of them in private homes—the men—in the rundown hotels, struggling with calefonts and air vents— were dead beat but most found it impossible to sleep. In the city centre it was airless: some of the hotels did not even have fans. Dilapidated trams squealed round corners late at night and began again soon after four in the morning. The intense heat on top of all the hospitality hardly helped. Those members billeted in private homes found their hosts keen to chat into the small hours. "They were amazed at the tales of English hardship during the war," one said. "Some even cried."

But the greatest torment of all was the mosquitoes. Wrote Elsie Beyer:

I can only say that the Perth mosquitoes are flying elephants. They are enormous. It doesn't matter how much you plaster yourself with ointment and all the other anti-mosquito lotions. They have terrific dog-fights over your head and then dive bomb you . . . in fact I am quite sure that they rather like the stuff you put on and go off and tell their friends to come and have a good feed, because they increase in numbers as the night goes on. Most of us look as though we have got small-pox and speaking for myself I can only say that I have got the most enormous lumps all over which are slowly but very *surely* driving me mad.

Olivier awoke after an hour or two for the same reason. If he and Vivien were intent on buckling down to rehearsal all next day, their hosts thought otherwise: here was the chance of a lifetime to come into contact with legendary figures. So they had time only for a brief call in the morning: after lunch they took a quick swim at Scarborough Beach—this time a whole file of Perth's famed black swans flew high over their heads —and then on to a big party on the balcony of the Esplanade during which they succeeded (joked Olivier) in shaking hands with the whole of Perth. They met the Lieutenant-Governor, the Lord Mayor, the Premier of Western Australia. They met the Archbishop, the Minister of the Interior, the Chief Justice, the Chancellor of the University; the leading business men, doctors, bankers and lawyers.

Hats were the order of the day: Mercia Swinburne, dark-haired and brown-eyed, peeked out from under a wide-brimmed, off-the-face model of white felt; Elsie Beyer, quickly becoming known as "matron", sported a strange number of Breton straw tied with green cord. Vivien Leigh —much cooler now in white muslin—had added aquamarines to her other jewels.

Then again that evening they were entertained, when they met more people, and again the following day when they attended a production of *Oedipus* performed by students in a sunken garden in the University. Olivier made a little speech praising the production but critical of the acting: "Why is it," asked Michael Redington, writing to friends, "peculiar young men always take up acting?"

The following Saturday they were due to open *The School for Scandal* at a gala performance, so on Wednesday they were glad to get down to proper rehearsal, though "Sir Laurence wanted to rehearse all the time," complained a younger member. Australian Equity were wide-eyed because the actors received no extra money. The stage director, David Kentish, working on the set, did not even go to bed—though he kept himself well supplied with liquor.

The temperature still hovered at around 100 degrees but during Wednesday night a tropical deluge descended and they were amazed, on going to pre-dress rehearsal on Thursday, to find the wardrobe staff with trousers rolled up to their knees. The women had to strip off shoes and stockings, and join in baling out water from the dressing rooms. To prevent the wardrobe from being flooded brushes and mops were mobilised, and those costumes already wet had to be hung outside to dry. The three dress rehearsals Olivier had hoped to hold were cut down to two.

The lack of dressing-room space was solved by the Oliviers as follows: in Sheridan style, using screens, they partitioned off the prompt side of the stage and here everyone dressed together. Next to this, screened off by wire netting covered with a curtain, Vivien had her own little place. Olivier dressed in the wings on the OP (Opposite Prompt) side with nothing more than a chair, table, and piece of carpet. Switchboard facilities were poor but fortunately they had brought their own lighting board. However, given the Capitol's size the acoustics seemed an insurmountable problem, while the musical director, Harold Ingrams, rehearsing with a local orchestra, "a weird and strange collection of people", was not always getting the Handel-Beecham incidental music, *The Great Elopement*, quite right. "The dear orchestra," wrote Olivier to John Burrell in London, "are not capable of playing quietly, and the trumpeter has an incurable vibrato on a consistent quarter tone sharp—dear, dear, I fear Sir Thomas would not be pleased." Nor was Olivier who, from his early choral training, had retained a fastidious ear.

Olivier leapt about from stage to stalls delivering his own lines then checking lights and audibility. Some years earlier, in an eight-foot leap from a balcony in *Theatre Royal*, he had broken his ankle, and while on the *Corinthic* he had complained of gout in his toe. Now the wardrobe had made the costume shoes he wore as Teazle too small, and his right foot began to hurt badly again. So he had to hobble about on a stick, using Elsie to report to him from the auditorium. She, coming down from the gallery at the back, missed a step and fell down another dozen, blackening all one side of herself with bruises and hurting her knee.

Till midnight on the eve of the opening night Vivien worked sewing and ironing costumes. The union-conscious Australians marvelled at the antics of the Company—"working from 10 am to 11.30 pm"—while the latter were shocked by the degree to which the unions controlled all aspects of life in Australia: "We have our labour troubles at home," wrote Elsie Beyer, "but we are not bound hand and foot by labour as they are here." She referred to the unpopular policies of the British Chancellor of the Exchequer, Sir Stafford Cripps: yet the Australian Prime Minister greatly admired Cripps, once stating that a 150-foot monument to him ought to be erected overlooking the Thames.

When booking opened there had been a terrible rush for seats and by 9 am, outside a warehouse called Nicholson's in Barrack Street, a queue 120 yards long had formed. Before four the previous afternoon the first arrivals had taken up positions: among them sixty-three-year-old Mrs Tunney, who carried a folding chair for the night vigil. "It is more than thirty years since I saw a real London show," she wrote, but regretted they found nothing to entertain them during the night—"In London there was always a man with his monkey, a street singer or comedian."

Others in the queue had a round-the-clock rota organised, like M. W. Jarvis:

> Our schoolboy son—then aged fourteen—went into the city at 4 pm . . . as number 5 in the queue. At 6 pm my wife and niece relieved our son in spot number 5 until 9 pm. By this time the queue was half the length of one main street and around the corner for the full length of the next street. I took over number 5 at 9 pm—equipped with Thermos, stool and rug. It was quite a jovial line of people and a cause of much amusement to evening people in the city. About midnight when theatre people and strollers had mostly wended their

47

way homeward a large car pulled alongside the head of the queue and we all gasped as we identified who had alighted from the car. Sir Laurence Olivier and Vivien Leigh. They came across and spoke with great interest and pleasure to up about spot 7 or 8. Sir Laurence shook hands with me. The rest of the night passed so quickly.

Better than a man with a monkey! Mr Jarvis correctly identified the beginning of a new love affair for the universally famed lovers: between them and the people of Australia.

As director, Olivier had definite views about *School*, the only play they performed in Perth. He had a personal predilection for this period "whose style, atmosphere, behaviour, and theatrical modes and manners, I feel more comfortably at home in than any other". This view should be taken with a pinch of salt: his great capacity was to be perfectly at home in any stage play in which he performed. Much later in his life he described his portrayal of James Tyrone in Eugene O'Neill's *A Long Day's Journey into Night*—his last major stage role, in 1971—as "one of my autobiographical jobs". When he made his pronouncement on *School* he had, he said, "just left the stage after playing the scene of Sir Peter's second quarrel with Lady Teazle"—he had a chameleon tongue as well as its colouring.

He also made a plea for realism within the artificiality of the play's conventions: never must one, he insisted, try to "score" off Sheridan. "Sheridan's cunning and deceptive appearance of formal realism can usually be understood only after much acting experience, or, in rare instances, by an instinctive gift for the style." These comments on acting the play, published as preface to a limited folio edition of 1949—when this production opened in London at the New Theatre—illustrate Olivier's complete grasp of both the historical and psychological process of acting.

But the practical problems at the Capitol, Perth, were almost entirely unrelated to the acting; the main one consisted of matching up the scene changes to the music and making the timing completely efficient. In the crippling heat the cues had to be practised endlessly. Michael Redington wrote:

Vivien Leigh came into the wardrobe at three this afternoon and stayed till 10.30. Sir Laurence has been in the theatre all the time since he arrived. I cannot tell you what it is to work with them, nothing is too much trouble, they are both so full of energy. I think if they are going to get going on a show they would never stop unless they were made to.

But the other main problem was to prove even more serious.

At the Old Vic Company's first—and highly bizarre—encounter with 2,280 Australians the heat was still oppressively sultry but the cast, sweating in wigs and in Cecil Beaton's resplendent costumes, could not but ogle through every available crack at the side of the stage at the women in fur wraps. Every kind of outfit filled the house—to loud whirring from the air-cooling device. When the house stood to sing "God Save the King" the full range of incredible finery became apparent, forming a quite remarkable mixture of classlessness, sophistication, and provincialism. While the men had dressed in everything from open-necked shirts and summer suits to top coats and tails, the women—hair for most of them piled in high coiffs—were draped in daring off-the-shoulder gowns, billowing skirts, a jungle of varied fabrics, and other exotic frocking.

Silence. The air-cooling device whirred ominously. Then the State Governor, Sir James Mitchell—"a most extraordinary looking little man," said Eileen Beldon—arrived late with his wife. As they settled down two brilliantly attired flunkeys entered one from each side of the stage, stepping slowly and deliberately to Handel's music, to "light" the footlights, using tapers. This augured well, but the first scene at Lady Sneerwell's passed dully, neither Mercia Swinburne nor Oliver Hunter (as Snake), gaining much sympathy from the house. Fortunately Peter Cushing as Joseph Surface then made his entrance, seized the initiative, and never relinquished it. When he was joined by Terence Morgan as Charles his brother, then by Eileen Beldon as Mrs Candour, and Dan Cunningham as Sir Benjamin Backbite—at this point the play really beginning to show positive life—the actors became very nervous over the absolute silence that still greeted their efforts. When, at last, pockets of laughter were detected, they gave a sensation

of playing in a choppy sea, each commotion aroused can-
celling out another somewhere else in the acoustical
void.

The score was, wrote one reviewer next day, that "we were
all on our best behaviour, and didn't want to break up the
sequence of the play with bursts of clapping. And until they
print programmes in phosphorous ink, or emboss them with
braille, we're likely to be pretty clueless about the identity of
any heavily disguised character who totters on to the stage."
He referred to Olivier, in hat and heavy cloak, making his first
entrance which passed almost unnoticed and completely un-
applauded. The audience thought they had made a terrible
gaffe. When they did recognise him many felt cheated because
he had not appeared as himself but impersonating an irascible
"old stumping husband" (Olivier was experimenting with
make-up and conceded he might have made himself look too
old). "Character work" the *Perth Record*'s critic, aptly titled
"De Gustibus" (if his mood was anything to go by), called
it.

But no one could miss Vivien Leigh as Lady Teazle: she got
a tremendous round. De Gustibus said he would have liked to
have thrown a brick at the noisy air cooling fan. But he and
everyone else agreed that in spite of the problem of audibility
there was, as Raymond Bowers wrote in the Perth *Sunday
Times*, between Olivier and Leigh "so implicit a timing, so
mutual a give and take of nuance and point that it was a joint
triumph". Besides Cushing and Bernard Merefield (Crab-
tree), George Relph as Sir Oliver Surface and James Bailey as
Moses came in for special praise.

The Capitol was the true villain of the evening. Its bowels
ingested all sound. The seventh row of the stalls could hear
nothing but the back of the stalls heard all. Some voices did not
carry while others did. Olivier later wrote to John Burrell:

It was quite a task as you may imagine to bash over
Sheridan's gossamer trifle in a way that would be appreciated by 2,280 people . . . the entire company was roaring
and spurting out consonants like machine-gun fire . . .
however, the audience seems delighted—God bless them. It
is the first live show that has played in this theatre for ten

years, and I think a great deal of inaudibility that was complained of, is on account of their having forgotten how to listen.

Redington, who with John Barnard was "dressing" the men, observed how Olivier behaved backstage on the first night. "He was so calm . . . he seemed to have time for everybody. I wished him good luck, he said 'Thank you old boy'. I am convinced he doesn't know my name yet!" From the front of the house, Redington continued, the production looked

rather like a Pollock's Theatre . . . production that you can stop at any moment and it is a "picture". There is a great deal of movement in it, and there are one or two really excellent scenes, especially the screen scene: this is perfectly played and I think Vivien Leigh is giving a brilliant perform-ance as Lady Teazle, especially after the discovery. Sir Laurence is so good, the way he laughs at the joke of pulling away the screen and then turns and sees her to say "Lady Teazle, by all that's damnable!"

On subsequent nights the acoustics were improved by the concerted efforts of the engineering branch of the Postmaster-General's Department and specialists from the University to place microphones and loud-speakers on the stage and in the auditorium. In a curtain speech Olivier praised the "damned contrivance" that actually did now allow everyone—in every part of the theatre—to hear, though he "ruffled a few emu feathers" with a diatribe against microphones, which his audience took for granted. He later forcibly expressed the same dislike when he said they robbed audiences of their power over the actors on stage, because the actors could then dominate the audience without heeding their reactions.

Offstage, to the sex-hungry single young men, the girls of Perth appeared—after their skinny and underfed counterparts in London—delectable, with amazing breasts and legs and hips. "I was only just able to be a good boy, only just, I'm still panting," wrote Redington. But relations were demure and decent: restricted to dances and taking girls home in taxis; picnic lunches and grand receptions; tennis parties and bathing parties in a floodlit sea; outings in motor launches from the yacht club.

That second week in Perth passed very quickly. The Oliviers were subjected to the same punishing round of social engagements as in the first week, and though Olivier's socks and sandals at a cocktail party caused shivers among the well-groomed women, he shrugged these off saying he still had had no time to buy summer clothes. Vivien christened a new boat, naming it *Sabina*. One day 3,000 people gathered outside the Council Chambers where they had been invited to a cocktail party. Elsie Beyer, who found rather less to do than she had originally expected—Olivier and Vivien had engaged an Australian secretary, Floy Bell, to deal with all their local engagements on the tour—single-handedly tried to hold back the crowd. "Make way," she shouted like a majordomo, "make way for Sir Laurence and Lady Olivier." Hovering over them, possessive and protective, her presence was, they found, becoming a burden.

And rows between the Oliviers had broken out at night in Bellevue. At first their neighbours had been thrilled at the thought of living in close proximity to such famous people. But, reported Mollie Lyon,

> Their enthusiasm waned when each night after the show the Oliviers brought home a crowd of friends to partake of a meal and enjoy a noisy session into the small hours . . . The Oliviers' domestic differences, which were frequent, were conducted at a highly dramatic and theatrical level.

On Wednesday of week two an invitation to lunch for all the Company from the "Reelers Fraternity"—for short, "Reelers"—provided a mystery. Arriving at Perth's main Emporium Cafeteria, they were ushered up to the third floor. Who were these reelers? asked one of the Company. "Fishermen," whispered Vivien. "Cotton-operatives," countered

Eileen. "A select band of highland dancers," suggested someone else. "They could be alcoholics," joked Larry.

After a lunch of, in Eileen's words, "tepid lettuce and
steak"—but no drink—none was any the wiser when one of
their hosts rose, saying, "Pray silence for Sir Laurence
Olivier." Olivier had no idea that he had to make a speech but
he got to his feet and made a few off-the-cuff witticisms which
the Company, ill-at-ease and anxious, laughed at nervously,
though what he said was well above their hosts' heads.
Meantime the deafening clatter of crockery from the Emporium below continued and some of the Reelers noticed how Sir
Laurence appeared distinctly dejected.

As he sat down the MC rose again and this time so did all the
Reelers, booming out the Reeler's Anthem to a rousing tune:

> Fil'm up, Fil'm up
> It is our business

The startled Company could hardly believe their ears, and
began doubling up, holding their sides, or looking at one
another with bursting faces. The Reelers sang again the
chorus, "Fil'm up, Fil'm up!" and then at last it dawned on the
Company what they were: members of the motion picture
industry!

Olivier again rose and barely keeping a straight face, excused himself and the Company on the grounds that they had
to get back to the theatre. On the coach they collapsed,
shaking with laughter and singing the Reeler's Anthem while
Peter Cushing did imitations of the MC, and "Roses are
blooming in Picardy" (pronounced Pick-ar-dy), which the
Reelers had also sung.

If they had played *Richard III* in Perth as well as *School* they
could have filled the theatre for six weeks, but as it was they
played to capacity practically throughout and took £A15,000
at the box office. During the first eight days the Oliviers
personally received over 1,000 letters (in a city of just over
250,000 inhabitants), while one woman flew 2,000 miles from
Darwin just to see the show. Inspiring everyone on stage to do
their best, attending innumerable social functions and giving

interviews to press, radio and film companies ("wearing and nervous work", Olivier called it), they were proving outstanding leaders.

On two nights Olivier, because his foot again became inflamed, played Teazle with a stick and excluded himself from the dance at the end which he tapped out with his stick. Most other performances went without a hitch:

> [March 27th] My foot quite well now and I am dancing in the play instead of my would-be lame old man act which I was rather enjoying. Matinée. Speech getting quite Sheridanesque. "Truly, ladies and gentlemen a little laughter from the mouths of babes and sucklings is very heartening on a hot afternoon like this" (for the kids in front). Show getting better. Vivien loosening up no end . . . My make-up is still lousy . . . I've got a great deal to do on Sir P.

Vivien had been impeccable, "doing frightfully well," as Olivier said, "and making the most delicious contributions of a few bewitching little words here and there." They even found the energy to give a midnight swimming party at Scarborough Beach for the Company after two performances on Easter Monday. "Everywhere they went they both looked so heavenly," exclaimed their Australian secretary, Floy Bell. "They expected a certain amount of adulation but nothing like what they received."

So, like fabled lovers in some romance of old, they were mobbed by crowds and garlanded with flowers wherever they went, while all through their last performance clapping and cheering punctuated their lines. At the curtain call the cast, disconcerted to find they knew the words better than their enraptured audience, sang "Waltzing Matilda". "You have spoilt us—you have given us a bonzer time," declared Olivier in a speech.

Crowds milled about outside the Capitol, blocking William Street, climbing all over the airport bus which had come to pick up the Company, and singing "Auld Lang Syne". Police had to fight to clear a path for Olivier and Vivien to board their taxi, and as they entered it, Vivien for a moment standing on the running-board, her brilliant green eyes and freckles noted by an onlooker, they were cheered. Even at the airport, at midnight, an unusually large crowd had gathered. Up to the very last moment of departure they were making them sign autograph books and theatre programmes.

PART TWO

End of Summer

War is a pleasure compared to what faces us now—trying to build up a peacetime with you in the middle of it.

Antrobus in *The Skin of Our Teeth*

1 Adelaide

At Perth airport the Company split into two groups. Twenty-six left at midnight in a Trans-Australian Airline Skymaster; another twelve thirty minutes later in an Australian National Airlines Skymaster. Some of those in the first plane, after rehearsing *Richard III* in the morning, and performing *School* in the evening, had drunk too much wine at that night's swimming party and played in the surf with a rugger ball. They felt queasy as well as exhausted. Some had never flown before. But after a meal they began egging on their pilot to beat the other plane carrying the VIPs to Adelaide, and did so by flying at 11,000 feet.

In the smaller group Terence and Georgina Morgan, who had also never flown, found themselves at the rear without tip seats. It was a brilliant night and, flying at only 7,000 feet over the apparently endless Nullabor Plain, they could gain a fair impression of the cruel and sandy terrain where only stunted blue-bush and salt-bush grew, and where temperatures remained for months on end at 114-120 degrees. The sole annual supply of rain would descend over several days and vanish into the loose spongy soil and sandstone, forming a huge arterial system of rivers which connected to reservoirs—all underground.

Nocturnal by habit, Vivien was alert and in her element. She had undressed and changed into a pale blue négligé; with her porcelain complexion from which she had scrupulously removed all make-up, she looked, according to Georgina, "beautiful, absolutely divine". She made no attempt to sleep. Olivier, exhausted on his tipped seat, tried to, dozing off fitfully. The rest, crumpled in suits or dresses, restless and uncomfortable after the rush of departure, snatched the odd hour or so of slumber.

"Here's the sunrise!" Vivien cried out, waking up the whole plane—and indeed there was the most unforgettable sight many had ever beheld. The absolutely straight Perth-Adelaide railway line—stretching for 330 miles without a single bend —stood out as a small feature in its magnificence. Some of the men thought they were in fairyland: with Vivien, their fairy princess, exquisitely featured and with lipstick now in place, eager for arrival at the airport.

Adelaide, though sunny like Perth, was not quite so hot, but still quite a multitude turned out early to welcome the Company and catch glimpses of Olivier and Vivien as they drove from the airport to the South Australian Hotel. With the throng at their departure—the crowd at Perth airport being as large as one "extending from the Globe to Piccadilly" said Elsie—and with enthusiastic waving here at the other end, the image of a royal drive was further strengthened. In their spacious suite in the hotel Olivier and Vivien found the ante-room crammed with flowers.

Interrupted only by the flight across the desert the crippling social round began again. Press Conference at noon. Sir Laurence holds a pineapple. "Vivvy" tries our grapes. Sir Laurence reflects: "I believe in the theatre because it is the most ready and acceptable glamouriser of thought—and if we had more thought in the world there would be a lot less trouble." More photographs. Olivier manages to keep his good humour even when his chair collapses under him. Lunch. Courtesy visit to the Governor of South Australia, Sir Willoughby Norrie. Call at Theatre Royal—only one hundred yards away from hotel—to look at stage. Much reassured here: eighty-year-old theatre seating 1,450, with good flying and storage space backstage, and reasonable dressing-rooms—like a large Criterion. Quick sleep. Early dinner, then along to theatre to work until 1.30 am . . . Back to hotel, drink and chat . . .

They had rehearsed *Richard III* nearly every day in Perth: "Run through *Richard* in afternoon with foot up," had recorded Olivier in his diary on March 22. Popular demand would have supported a season of ten weeks in Adelaide but they were due to play only two. On the Friday morning before their Saturday night opening, with all preferential seats already sold, queueing for gallery seats began, continuing for twenty-six hours. On Saturday afternoon they held a final dress rehearsal, and then came the moment all had been waiting for—*Richard III*'s gala opening. Outside the theatre in Hindley Street 3,000 people gathered to watch the audience arrive and to get a glimpse of the Oliviers, while police estimated that another 5,000 filed past (Adelaide's whole population then was less than half a million).

Given the proximity of their hotel to the theatre the Oliviers could, to their own undisguised relief, slip unseen by anyone through the stage door. Vivien dressed anyhow while Olivier didn't need to touch up—for press photographers—his own complexion which of recent years, under the attrition of lights and stage make-up, had become poor.

The show opened to "boiled shirts"—as a junior member of the Company put it—row upon row of solid-looking, expensively turned-out South Australians who wondered if, at a guinea a seat, they had not all rather been taken for a ride on the advance publicity. But they sat in absolute silence, unified in high expectation. None of them thought much of the theatre —as one described it, a "dowdy sort of barn"—and many felt embarrassed that such a famous pair should have to act in such a dump. Yet Olivier thought otherwise, calling it, "quite divine".

Richard III, directed by John Burrell, had originally opened at the New Theatre on 26 September 1944. Olivier, who did all the lighting for the tour himself (though John Sullivan had done the original plot), spent many hours making sure that Doris Zinkeison's costumes should emerge at their most luminous from the background of Morris Kestleman's picturesque toy buildings. Olivier also improved considerably in other ways on the 1944 production, with which he now expressed dissatisfaction: in particular by casting George Relph in place of Nicholas Hannen as Buckingham, and substituting Peter Cushing for Relph as Clarence, he sharpened the characterisation and introduced many new and exciting moves.

But many particulars of the original had not been modified: Olivier kept Jane Shore's seductive passage across the stage; also retained was the appearance of Anne—now played by Vivien—in the coronation scene, sitting immobile at the side of the stage—a haunting prolepsis of Richard's malign intention

Come hither, Catesby; rumour it abroad
That Anne, my wife, is very grievous sick—

and of her own end.

If *Oedipus* at the New had been Olivier's first experience of
dropping exaggeratedly false traits of personality and leg-
padding—appearing as if naked and unashamed before an
audience—his earlier appearance as Richard had been the first
real taste of having his love for a character, only recently
stimulated by Guthrie, reciprocated by the audience.

As I turned [leftwards] to face them, my heart rose to
embrace this communion as to the miraculously soft
warmth of a rapturous first night of love.

Olivier had based the nastiness he projected on the director
Jed Harris, with whom he had worked in New York. Disney's
big bad wolf provided the lean and buoyant suggestiveness of
movement. On Adolf Hitler, too, as an incarnation of evil,
Olivier drew imaginatively. But the director, John Burrell,
though never mentioned in this connection, also influenced
him: with irons on one leg, a surgical boot on the foot of the
other, Burrell, in daily contact with Olivier, supplied a living
example of someone continuously and tenaciously rising
above his physical disability. Burrell could also be a fearful
practical joker.

But if he had assembled "from the outside in"—as he
described his method of approach—a wonderful selection of
electrifying elements, how had Olivier completed his portrayal of Richard, becoming the character himself? Love, of
course, was the key. A kind of transformation of self-love:
"You accumulate a mass of new mannerisms and ways of
doing things," Olivier stated many years later on the Dick
Cavett Show in 1980:

Then from all of this detail you begin to sort out those things
that seem to be true to the character you've been forming as
you accumulated them. Things begin to emerge that in their
turn help you reinforce and expand the character. And since
it is really you, you begin to love this new side of your own

Free with the Argus every Saturday!

character as you have loved the old side. Possibly you love it more, since it is all so new and different, yet still you. This is still working from the outside in, but in a much more substantive way than most actors do it, which is simply to impose their own beings on the characters. This way, you let the character eventually impose himself on your own being.

Enormous pressures had gone into that extraordinary, and first, total realisation of character Olivier achieved with Richard: his many setbacks with Vivien, the frustration of his ambition through war and other, more ordinary factors; his burning sense of competition with Wolfit, Gielgud and others, making him reach for something extra in his achievement. But the greatest pressure of all had been the inner one, his need for love, and his need to give love. It was, then, even as far back as the original first night of *Richard* in 1944, that he had made it evident that he was beginning to fall in love with the characters he played on stage more strongly than his—already half-fictionalised—love for Vivien. Probably he was never wholly conscious of this. But it was only in the relative harmony of the tour that Vivien had a chance to see and understand the change that had taken place inside him. For nearly four years she had not recognised any such change but from now on she had to confront it. Its realisation, in the clear Australian light that so dazzled the eyes of these visitors, shook her own confidence in him.

Many critics have held that Richard III was Olivier's best and truest part: Kenneth Tynan spoke for them when he said that in Richard "the two sides of Olivier's nature met and married in one supreme coalition". Therefore it is tempting to claim that of all the parts he played it was nearest to his own real character. Yet what an actor or artist can best project or suggest need not be what he is, and although there has been much in Olivier's personality of the Machiavellian—in the best sense, as in Machiavelli's *The Prince*, an exemplary tract on good leadership—many diametrically opposed traits to Richard's existed. His tender-heartedness to those with whom he worked is but one instance of the endearing sides of this complex man.

Yet his mind, instinctively, always moved impressionisti-
cally with the shallow rapid pace of Shakespeare's Richard,
and had always been prone to underline the comic, the bizarre,
the nakedly unashamed or the ruthless. His capacity being for
quickness, energy, violence, unexpectedness, he never had
any great depth or sensitivity. The emotional level at which
Shakespeare, not yet quite at his maturity as a poet, pitched
Richard III found its exact response from Olivier in his
maturity.

Marshalling all sides of his skill in a perfect blend of the
outer and inner man, he never showed greater versatility,
power, or concentration than as Richard. "I don't think
anything quite touched his Richard," said Sybil Thorndike.
"One of the most sexually attractive characters ever to disgrace the stage," said Terence Rattigan. Richard became real
as Olivier was real.

Above all as Richard he flaunted a quality that he has always
demonstrated in full measure, both on and off stage, but which
had, up to 1948—and though very English—rarely been
remarked on: a supreme love of bad taste.

Reviewing the Australian opening C. R. Jury, Professor of
English at Adelaide University, confirmed how Olivier, in
1948, still showed not only Shakespeare's imagination at
work, but also his thought. In another review Mary Armitage
referred to him as "Hell's black intelligencer". "Olivier gave
us so many facets of the dark complexities of Richard,"
declared the *Adelaide Mail*'s critic, "that one felt almost a
physical weariness when the curtain fell at the finale." Backstage, Michael Redington noticed Olivier—the actor Mac-
ready had done something similar—shaking the iron ladder
leading to the electrics board, to gear up all his strength.

The fight at the end included two innovations, the first
unintentional, the second—though unrehearsed—more
calculated. A foot from the point, Olivier's sword snapped,
sending the blade flying across the stage where it narrowly
missed some men-at-arms. Replacement by a dozen hands
offering swords was made so quickly that some people felt the
whole manoeuvre was deliberate.

The second innovation was more in keeping with Edmund
Kean whose picture often stood on Olivier's dressing-room

table. In his death paroxysms Olivier, remembering what his great predecessor had done, suddenly pointed his sword and threw it at Dan Cunningham.

Was this unconsciously a jealous gesture? Olivier may well have harboured murderous thoughts towards his Richmond who was, it seemed to everybody in the Company, enamoured of Vivien.

An old boy of the Scottish public school Fettes, Cunningham had played rugger for Waterloo and just before the war worked for a Shanghai and Hong Kong bank in Liverpool, leaving it to join the local repertory company. Commissioned in the Seaforth Highlanders, he was captured after Dunkirk, and spent the next five years in POW camps. Here he often entertained in "Oflags", trying unsuccessfully to escape on several occasions. But ultimately his war experience had badly scarred him, for during his imprisonment his wife had gone off with another man, and on his return he found his home neglected, his suits blasted with mildew.

He played Richmond with the ex-serviceman's lustre of a true Brit: according to Professor Jury, "the very personification of a clean-up". With his natural fine blond hair and noble face, he looked in many ways, especially in the stage fight, more at ease in the part than Ralph Richardson, his predecessor in London. But inwardly, his Richmond apart, Cunningham had little confidence.

Not that Cunningham's attachment to Vivien was, at this stage, serious—or taken seriously in the Company. It was not unusual for men to fall in love with Vivien, and she kept a small token court of admirers. The Cleopatra side of her personality—which could be kittenish and cruel—made a game of luxuriating in their glances and she dispensed easily, in very theatrical style, hugs and kisses. The scenic artist and chief flyman, Roger Ramsdell, a gnarled, good-humoured, white-haired old fellow with a love of the bottle, who doubled for part of the trip as personal cook to the Oliviers, in particular came in for much affectionate raillery. The sight of Vivien laughing and flirting with this much older man shocked the younger women.

As Lady Anne, the "malevolent toad's" wife, she excelled

—the very image of trampled-on beauty. "Beautiful and touching", the critics found her: or, "beautiful and pathetic". But she thought the small part boring and killed time in her dressing room by playing gin rummy or reading detective novels (Simenon in particular). Like Olivier she had begun to tire of the social round: already in Perth they had disagreed about having to attend a lecture at the University—"She makes the most damn awful fuss," Olivier noted in his diary. In Adelaide they had even more social engagements. Olivier kept on at her to improve Lady Teazle, critical of her woodenness and insisting she needed to bubble more at the end with both "inner and audible" laughter.

The problems grew. Olivier was finding scope for his larger-than-life ambition and heroic energy which, as he later said in a radio tribute to Ralph Richardson, would have turned to criminality had he not found a scale of endeavour equal to them. Not only was he growing into a brilliant leader of the Company, he was also beginning to relax and find humour in the role: Terence Morgan recalled being in an Adelaide taxi with him when crowds had formed along the route and when, as they passed, the women curtsied and the men raised their hats. "There you are, my boy," Olivier said, turning to him, "there's your great actor."

Vivien too, in this respect inspired by him, adopted the role of the sympathetic and astute leading lady. Together, with their example, they got the best out of every member of the Company and in order to do this did not spare themselves. While in real life neither was much of a father or mother to their children of former marriages, in that simplified, though dangerous and unstable, substitute world of theatre they played the parts beautifully, possibly because the commitment was of a different kind—external, emotional, essentially false because only temporary. To every member of the Company they sent a little poem:

> Members of the Co
> Please to let us know
> When your birthdays are,
> Be they near or far,
> So that we may wish you

All that fate can dish you.
Otherwise there is no mirth
In remembrance of your birth.
A lonely birthday is no joko,
And we "Parentis" are "in loco".
We also love you very dearly
And are always yours sincerely.
Bye Bye V. L. Hello L. O.

They carried out their attentions with great care and spirit; but at Notley the previous autumn one of the Company had been quite staggered to hear Vivien apologising on the phone to her fifteen-year-old daughter for having forgotten her birthday.

Vivien, a delicate figurehead with whom everyone was "in love", and with whom everyone wanted to be seen, had, however, none of the managerial keenness Olivier had developed. And working from instincts and emotions she could always switch mood dangerously and unexpectedly. Those who got on with her, or worked for her, while acknowledging her great sense of fun, were always conscious how carefully they needed to tread. Suddenly, if she misunderstood something, she could turn and become very frightening. Her expression would harden quite inexplicably, her eyes would change colour.

In Adelaide she was still on a reasonably even keel. She kept her smoking down to ten cigarettes a day (both she and Olivier smoked Du Mauriers). She loved chocolates. But she had to live on a "high" or not at all. The destructive side of her sought an outlet.

She had identified an enemy in the Company. There was only one woman temperamentally strong enough to stand up to her. Someone who, as well, seemed constantly to disapprove of her. She had to "live it up" after the show. But that other woman was there, hovering about constantly at Larry's side. And while Vivien needed excitement he just wanted to go to bed.

They all joked in the Company about Elsie Beyer's protectiveness, saying you could tell her mood by the shades in the

glasses: "Pitch black today," they would say. She was the odd
woman out. The Company as a whole considered her a
killjoy. Vivien would show scorn by repeating her name in
separate syllables, placing her emphasis on the first syllable of
the surname, on the next raising her eyebrow and comically
lifting and lightening her voice. She would bide her time, and
then persuade Larry to get rid of her.

In Adelaide the innocence and novelty of being King and
Queen wore off. But for their Australian admirers that innocence and novelty had hardly dimmed, for admiration of stars
is by its very nature a platonic love, and the pair represented
some ideal which a less material age might try to represent in
art or myth but which in this new era had to be seen, touched,
and photographed. Mrs E. M. Fisher of Parkholme, South
Australia, wrote of *Richard III*:

> I do *not* remember who played the other parts, but I
> remember Olivier—such is fame . . . some inkling of
> Olivier's performance and its strength may be gained from
> the fact that all these thirty-four years and married life and
> three children later, I still remember his whisper on the stage
> which rose above the tiers and danced about the air above
> us.

Constance Radcliffe remembered also the first night of
Richard III:

> I am now seventy-five years and will always remember that
> night rather like the book on the *Titanic* when it sank.

She had queued all day for the last performance and would
have got no tickets, but because someone returned some,
found herself with a seat right at the back of the gallery:
"Allergic to heights . . . I was in a bath of perspiration and
scarcely able to speak." All that soon changed. The moment
she enjoyed most was when

Richard called for some ale and then didn't wait for it and when the servant appeared with a large glass of Australian beer (much lighter in colour than English) he stood for a few moments and there was dead silence in the theatre and then he up and drank it himself, replaced the glass on the tray and there was still dead silence and then he let out a terrific belch which could be heard all over the theatre!

Gillian Thomas, a more youthful devotee of the Oliviers, at that time attended Girton Girls' School: "My friend Margie and I dared to go into the South Australian Hotel and walked up to the floor where the Oliviers were staying. A maid offered to let us peep into their room (they were not there at the time of course, being, I think, at a matinée). Our excitement was indescribable . . . having actually sighted their dressing gowns hanging behind the door."

Back in their hotel after the show the Oliviers played a few tricks, too. They had asked that Terence and Georgina Morgan have a room opposite theirs and one night the Morgans, tired after the show, were sharing a bath. Suddenly they were startled to hear a loud knock on the bathroom door and an officious Australian voice drawling out, "Two people aren't allowed in the bath together!" They sat up guiltily, thinking, "Oh Christ, in this strange country anything's possible," and Morgan found himself calling out huffily, but feeling very foolish—"But we're man and wife!" There was a pause. A few moments later there was another, much lighter tap. "This is the housekeeper here," tittered a second Australian voice—at which point they realised it was Vivien.

At the theatre one night Olivier told the story of his investiture at Buckingham Palace to some of the Company. The King said to him (Olivier imitating his stutter), "The l-l-l-last time I saw you you weren't b-b-b-blond . . ." "No," Olivier replied, "I have dyed my hair as I am playing Hamlet, a Dane." The King knighted him, then saying, "Arise Sir Francis Day." (Frances Day was a music hall artiste—with dyed blond hair.)

The most droll of their numerous engagements in Adelaide was a packed gathering at the Town Hall when, on their arrival with the Company, the acting Lord Mayor of Adelaide introduced them as "Sir Olliver and Lady Leigh"—to horrified gasps from the audience. Sometimes Leigh would be pronounced as "Lay"; but neither she nor Olivier was allowed by the British Council to be interviewed on radio, a ban incomprehensible to most Australians who blamed it on the newspapers.

On their second Saturday in Adelaide, after two shows of *Richard III*, the Oliviers gave a party for Peter and Helen Cushing to mark their fifth wedding anniversary, at which everyone ate oysters and drank until 3.45 am. Meantime, the stage staff were at work all night dismantling *Richard* and putting up in its place the set of *The Skin of Our Teeth*, which, because of its size required them to enlarge the orchestra pit. They found driving nails into the stage floor of jarrah (ironwood) very difficult.

Straight from his party Olivier got down to lighting *Skin*, at once hitting a terrible problem as none of the plot they had used at the Piccadilly Theatre would apparently fit the Adelaide stage. Desperation mounted until he and Bill Bundy, the chief electrician, solved the problem by realising that whoever had transcribed the plot had the Prompt and OP corners of the stage the wrong way round. "Could it be H. M. Tennent's spite against the Old Vic?" asked Olivier, who was by now excessively nervous.

The second week in Adelaide totally centred on Vivien Leigh (although Olivier had taken over the role of Mr Antrobus), and was probably the happiest of the tour. But it began, on Sunday night, with freak weather: a storm of hurricane proportions uprooted huge trees in city squares and parks, taking the roofs off houses. At the resort of Glenelg, six miles away, where the original British settlers landed from HMS *Buffalo* in 1836 (in a curtain speech Olivier flatteringly told his audience he was sure no convicts had come to Adelaide), the jetty was swept away as easily as a matchbox. A RAN survey ship, HMAS *Barcoo*, was tossed up on the beach like a cork.

By Monday fine weather had re-established itself in time for the opening which had, much to Olivier's terror, been moved forward a day. But *The Skin of Our Teeth* went magnificently, everyone agreeing that Vivien's Sabina had greatly improved

Original programme drawing by Loudon Sainthill.

since her performance at the Piccadilly. At the end it got a wonderful reception, after which Vivien made just the right speech in which she congratulated Adelaide on its reaction and paid tribute to Olivier's production: "A *very* good *long* speech," according to Olivier, though he remained unhappy with his "uneven and unfinished" performance as Antrobus, and with the "break-up bits" of the play. "I wanted to play the part so much I hate to be disappointing myself in it."

In *Skin*, as the *femme fatale* recurrent in the history of mankind, Vivien appeared first as the Antrobus's maid (Antrobus = Anthropos = man—heavy symbolism); next as a bathing beauty; then as an army camp follower; and finally, again, as the maid. Undoubtedly she made the role her own by being both sexually fascinating and intellectually stimulating. In turn satirical, vibrant, and touching, she could—using her gifts to their best advantage—switch rapidly from mood to mood.

Like both Leslie Caron and Brigitte Bardot she had trained as a ballet dancer and so as the bathing belle she proved a delight to the audience's senses, displaying—as far as decency allowed—her enticing body with brazen and coquettish style. Many Australians, touchingly naive in response to what they saw, were quite amazed that Olivier should allow his wife to act such a trollop. They could not understand, either, how he, married to Vivien, could kiss Eileen Beldon (Mrs Antrobus).

Though a first-rate vehicle for Vivien, *Skin* was a work of oddly mixed styles. Olivier called it the "Picasso of our repertoire": at another time the "Henry Moore", or the "Salvador Dali". Most of Thornton Wilder's language could be identified as pastiche of everything from *Hellzapoppin* to *Finnegans Wake*. The characters behaved as cardboard cut-outs, deliberately conceived to flout form and meaning. The play divided its Australian audience into two camps: those who with unnecessary humility found it above their heads, and those who became carried along by its undeniably vital ragbag of styles and unorthodox vaudeville presentation, something they had never experienced before. But no one considered it especially profound.

The Company was highly relieved it went down so well. So

there was nothing much else for them to do before they left Adelaide on 18 April but become thoroughly boozed on a visit to Stonyfell vineyard, where they witnessed the crushings and "sampled all and sundry [noted Olivier] and though the sherry was very good . . . we dared not enjoy it as we should have liked". A flagon of sherry given to the Oliviers shattered in the gutter outside the Art Gallery when their car door opened too hastily. From Adelaide Olivier was sent off with a gift from the male staff of the theatre of an ink-stand of rare burraburra wood, while Vivien received from the female contingent a huge box of chocolates. On account of her continuous vitality the press nominated her "Miss Vitamin B". Olivier recorded in his diary, "V is wonderful—better than ever." For the first time on the tour she could at last feel her own stature to be the equal of his.

2 Melbourne

In Perth people asked, recalled the actor Thomas Heathcote, "What'll you have?" In Adelaide, "What's your religion?" In Melbourne, "What family do you come from?"—while in Sydney, most bluntly of all, "What have you got?" Certainly the Company enjoyed most the first two cities, for hospitality was offered at a more personal level, while the cities themselves, being old-fashioned, colonial in structure, and still looking towards "home", were immensely flattered to be visited by the "Theatre royals". All particularly loved their stay in Adelaide. But the novelty had inevitably palled: now in Melbourne they were due for an eight-week engagement, playing all three plays.

Their arrival in the "Holy City" augured badly. They had

boarded a midnight train and no one could sleep. A lot were becoming very homesick. When they detrained it was raining; many hated the accommodation they had been found and spent the first couple of days trying to change it. Bernard Merefield, the oldest actor among them but who still collected train numbers, fell ill with shingles; John Barnard got bad asthma and could not sleep. Elsie Beyer increasingly worried about the Oliviers' health. To cheer himself up Dan Cunningham went off to have a shirt made but found the tailor proposed, owing to the shortage of labour, taking two months over it. Terence Morgan was photographed huddled in a duffel coat—in Australia a sartorial innovation. Michael Redington in a letter home reflected with youthful shortsightedness,

> The awful thing about Australia is that one can see no hope for them, they are so union-ridden, and have such a lack of individuality, that there seems no chance for their people. Their Prime Minister is a boiler-man and the Governor-General [William McKell, an ex-boilermaker] not much better. So it just shows, people are dreading what will happen when the King and Queen [due to tour Australia in 1949] come, being left in the hands of this man!*

But Olivier and Vivien arrived in Melbourne in cracking form. They had travelled on their own, crossing, as Vivien described it, "the most wonderful country imaginable . . . great shallow blue lakes surrounded by glistening white sand, black and white branches of trees sticking out of water and birds of every kind and description everywhere". After motoring through the great forests they booked in for the night at Jens Hotel, Mount Gambier, under the names "Mr and Mrs Laurence". Even the proprietor, a Mr J. O'Connor, did not guess that Mr and Mrs Laurence were "of more interest" than other tourists. (By this time Mr and Mrs Laurence heartily wished they were not.)

Their night here passed strangely, according to Vivien, who

* Perhaps the best-known joke at the time was made by Robert Menzies who, when Chifley rose in Parliament and asked, "Mr Speaker, what is before the 'ouse?" stood up and said, "An 'h' usually."

wrote to Hugh Beaumont in London: "The midnight clock struck eighteen and the fire alarm was set off every two hours just to see if the poor old thing was alright (and that we knew it)." After calling at the birth-place of their great friend Robert Helpmann where they took photographs—"always high mountains [recorded Olivier] and always cream, dirty ochre and black dairy cattle in foreground. But never never no kangaroos" (they had in fact seen white kangaroos so far only at Adelaide in a private collection)—they then spent Sunday on the beach, eight miles from Mount Gambier. On Monday, motoring to Melbourne, Olivier smelt burning rubber while the speedometer dropped to 40 mph; in Camperdown they stopped and finding a tyre had burned right down to the rim, changed it.

It proved fortunate for them—and for the Company—that they did have this break: Melbourne was out to get them. At the press conference were enough reporters to cover the job effectively for all the papers in Australia, while the mood revived memories of wartime coldness towards Britain. Yet it quickly passed, Helen Seager writing in the *Argus* (21 April), "Never, Ma'am, and I mean NEVER, in a long and somewhat disillusioning career, have I ever seen the men and women of the Press fall so heavily, hook, line and sinker, for the charm of a couple they were all keyed up to resent."

Olivier's apparent humility worked this transformation. The woman from the *Herald* observed him "in the flesh" as being "slightly different from Olivier on the screen—younger in spite of a touch of grey in the brown hair at the temples", and she listed his four pet hates as: "Shaving; small-talk; taking off make-up; making [radio] recordings."* Another woman fell into rapturous description of Vivien's "small, tip-tilted nose, and her curving mouth . . . the tiny, elusive dimple at the edge of her chin", while noting her dislikes as "slacks, except on tall women, seeing herself in films, short skirts". They loved her sharp, almost autocratic, English accent: "a clear soft voice . . . [showing] an ear that must be well nigh

---

* Was the ban on radio due to Olivier's thinking he had a poor radio voice? He certainly recorded as little as he could.

perfect. No 'Oxford' accent, no exaggerated emphasis—instead, clear enunciation and beautifully modulated tone." Olivier commented: "Vivien carried the wretched thing off with superlative charm," adding with an almost audible sigh, "a wearing hour and a half".

Such a fanfare at their first Melbourne reception once again proclaimed them in their most demanding role as the Great Lovers—which must have eaten at the heart of their affection. In front of the cameras they gazed at one another with misty eyes, praised one another in just the right tone of adoration. The men fell for Vivien, the women for Olivier: who could fail to be captivated—or intoxicated? But privately they grew near exhaustion point.

Their old matron Elsie was getting desperately worried about it, and at the end of April discussed with Dan O'Connor what they should do. "Couldn't they have a break?" she asked him, while he replied that he would think about it. They looked exhausted all the time, crawling off to bed whenever they were not required for a performance or for some civic engagement. Vivien started running a temperature and missed five performances in a week. Petite and pretty—and a first-rate replacement—Georgina Jumel took the role of Sabina, much encouraged by Olivier who, after a quick run-through to test her lines, sent round oysters with brown bread and butter to her dressing room before the show. She did magnificently well, although the audience was furious at being cheated of Vivien. Olivier himself went down with a bad throat and had to cancel several performances ("I assure you that it was not I who laid my husband low," Vivien told listeners at a party).

While the reviews of *School* and *Richard III* had been excellent and while queues outside the theatre were just as long as in Adelaide, with, in the words of one reporter, "seething pre-performance lobby scena calling to mind nothing so strongly as sheep-dipping scenes in the great outback", backbiting and antagonism towards *Skin* grew in the press. One critic whom Redington met at a party complained that the Company might as well have done *Charley's Aunt*.

All this had a dispiriting effect but Olivier kept up morale with an understudy rehearsal at which, in one act, he played

Antrobus drunk, and in the next gave a superb imitation of John Gielgud. He repeated this imitation during an actual performance, prancing about the stage, and speaking in a high voice, recounted Redington. "When he had to say 'For God's sake shut up' he yelled out at the top of his voice, just like John G. in an emotional scene." In another performance, at the beginning of Act III when Antrobus enters saying "Seven of our actors have been taken ill", Olivier reappeared in a ravishing juvenile make-up with glossed hair so as to get an entrance round of applause and "to dry Vivien up, which he did".

His popularity with the Company increased even more during a performance of *Richard* after the four bearers had carried him dead to centre stage (and just before the famous death throes). One of the four, Michael Redington, trod on his wig; "Dead, he gave a terrific shout and played his death throes with his hand on his forehead! He was wonderful about it afterwards and said he knew it wasn't on purpose but if it happened again they must gather round him until he can put it on again." But most popular of all was his announcement, after one performance at the beginning of May, "Elsie thinks we're all very tired, and she's bloody right. So we're having a week's holiday in Tasmania, after the next stage of the tour."

But they still had to get through the rest of May and most of June. Redington wrote of dinner dates following lunch dates with bewildering consistency. "I have cut out evening parties, though. I have learnt my lesson and they are just a bit too much. You find you never have any chance to regain your lost sleep." Olivier also revealed his feelings when he wrote to John Burrell of Melbourne's mood of receiving them:

Piss-elegant and nervously smug at first. There's a great feeling of tense humourless fear that one is getting at them all the time. It makes it all rather a strain—to say the least . . . Of course I was expecting the worst before I left, but . . . sometimes this job seems a bit harder than I thought it could be. A fortnight ago the Premier of Victoria and the Cabinet gave us all a lunch (v. much the Premier—Mr Holloway) and the inevitable speeches followed it of course

78

—well I said all really that I was able to cough up, without shaming myself by repeating too much from the hundreds of others I had done in front of the company. We were then carted all round the houses of Parliament and met all their wives—The President and the Speaker called for hush and I realised that another epic was descending upon me. As all the people from the lunch were there I couldn't for the life of me think of anything else to say! So I feebly and desperately made a joke of it and got a cheap laugh with some Australian slang—Every day dear boy *every day* since, a controversy has raged in the press as to whether I was *insulting* them by using words like "bonzer" and "beaut" or not— wonderful?

Though he concealed it beneath the joky tone of his letter to Burrell, Olivier knew his own desperate fatigue: remembering only the disagreeable side he later wrote:

As we reached the more sophisticated cities, they seemed to become progressively less enthusiastic, seemingly inclined to sit back as if saying "All right, then, show us". Melbourne gave us our first cool reception, one newspaper saying, "We have better Richard IIIs here in Melbourne' . . . So I thought, "That's very promising", and set out to make enquiries. There turned out to be, after the most diligent search, no professional actors working in Melbourne, and it was hard to believe that amateur groups would have the money required for such ambitious productions.

Olivier in fact did take talent-scouting seriously: while in Adelaide he had already auditioned Keith Michell, then on the arts staff of Adelaide Boys High School, who as a result came to England to study at the Old Vic School. But his memory of the Melbourne papers was faulty: of eight reviews of *Richard III* none had been less than glowing: phrases like "theatre at its best", "stirring drama", "feast of fine acting" were common. And in Melbourne, not only was Olivier overwhelmingly elected "Man of the Year for 1948" (by readers of the *Australasian Post*), but several newspapers devoted their leaders to extolling the results of the visit. For instance: "There can be no doubt that the Old Vic season has had an immense influence on the theatre-going public of Melbourne; it has given thousands of people a taste for the legitimate stage."

In spite of a lot of coughing at the first night of *Richard* which irritated Olivier, the response of the public was just as vehement. Mrs Sadie Enright recalled Melbourne in 1948 as being a "rather dingy, shabby place after the wartime austerity"—yet how terrific was the excitement when they heard that the "famous and beloved Vivien would be in Our Town". Of Vivien as Sabina she wrote:

> She was dressed as a maid in a cheeky short black dress with a frilly white apron, and tripped out flipping a feather duster. There was a large spiral type hat rack on stage, and as she dusted down the spirals, she gave a delicious giggle, and a flirty wriggle of the hips, rather like a little duckling. She enjoyed this caper so much, she stopped and paused and then did the whole thing again. The audience just loved it.

Mrs Patricia Carver found she "had a curiously light voice without any timbre. She did not really impress me as an actress." Mr Dinsmore of Brighton, Victoria, had a surgical instrument business; Vivien visited his shop three times for pedicures—"her toes were as pretty as her face." Helen Keller, the famous blind and deaf scholar who was on a world tour, sat in a box close to the stage at a performance of *Richard III*; her companion Polly Thomson interpreted the play to her with the aid of her own special finger language, and they, too, at the end of the performance received an ovation. Later when Miss Keller came to the dressing room Larry had lit a cigarette and did not know where to put it. At another time, a woman during an interval of *Richard III* was overheard saying, "And I understand the part was written specially for Sir Laurence."

Miss Judith Stump judged that *Richard* was "not perhaps the best choice for a display of *company* talent, but it was a marvellous vehicle for Olivier's virtuosity". At the head of an

The SS *Corinthic*. (*Below*) Olivier plunging into the canvas pool rigged up on deck.

Dan Cunningham (*left foreground*) eyed by Vivien, with Olivier sitting next to her, Captain Robinson standing behind and Elsie Beyer on right. (*Below*) Meeting the press in Fremantle. (*Opposite page*) Vivien as Sabina.

In Canberra on Anzac Day. (*Below*) Old Vic cricket team (*back row, l to r*) Bill Bundy, Peter Cushing, Michael Redington, Thomas Heathcote, Douglas Murchie, Earnest Phipps; (*front row*) Roy Hawkins, James Bailey, Tony Gavin, David Kentish.

In Tasmania: Cecil Tennant, Vivien and Olivier. (*Below*) Snapped on a beach near Brisbane, as seen by the *Sunday Telegraph*, Sydney.

HERE TOMORROW

SIR LAURENCE and Lady Olivier enjoying sun and surf at an Australian beach. In preparation for their Sydney season they rested last week. They arrive in Sydney tomorrow.

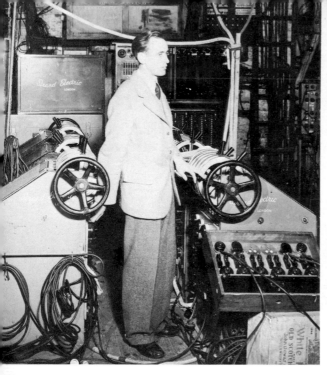

Bill Bundy (*top left*) with travelling hardware. (*Top right*) Anne McGrath and John Barnard in Brisbane Park. (*Below left*) Georgina Jumel and Terence Morgan. (*Below right*) Elsie Beyer.

Sir Peter and Lady Teazle. (*Below*) End of season mood in Brisbane.

(*Left*) Olivier with stick arriving in Sydney to play Richard III. (*Below*) Peeping from his canvas sling as he is hoisted aboard at Wellington for the journey home from New Zealand.

all-night queue on a wintry Sunday Miss Stump and her friend found themselves picked by the testy-voiced caretaker for a backstage tour. During this she suddenly became awesomely aware of "standing on the great stage", set for a performance of *Richard III*. After this she was ushered into Olivier's dressing room:

> The thing which I remember most clearly was the absolute order—nothing out of place. The make-up bench was clear, with sticks and tubes and jars all methodically arranged in trays. Hanging on the wall was a huge photo of Sir Laurence leaping from the parapet to murder Claudius, and on a table a presentation leather-bound volume of photographs from *Hamlet* presented to him by the cast.

The order was maintained by his shy dresser "Patty" Legh, a tiny, grey-haired widow who had lost both husband and son at sea and whose devotion to Olivier bordered on worship. Patty recalled how he had none of the usual theatrical superstitions—about using new sticks of greasepaint on a first night, not standing shoes on a chair, and whistling blithely in his dressing room: "About the only thing he really insists on is his cup of tea."

No monarch or president, observing punctilios without end and responding to them with wit or solemnity, had, in the evenings of his tour, to strip naked, reshape his appearance and go on display as a different person. But this had, for the Oliviers, now become the practice. It was a far cry from the time when actors were buried at night in unsanctified ground.

The incredible number of ceremonies they attended in Melbourne reached a climax one Sunday afternoon in the Town Hall when Olivier addressed an Empire Youth Rally. He told his audience of 3,000 young people that God's great blessing to the Empire was family life, and that today the family, headed by the English Royal family, meant more to the Empire than it had in any time in its history: "Not the least of the blessings . . . is Princess Elizabeth, a very great and conscientious human character, aware that some day she will be queen, to rule with the love of a mother, combined with the stomach and strength of an English King." With dignity and

emotion he then read Princess Elizabeth's 21st birthday dec-
laration: "I declare before you all that my whole life, whether
it be long or short, shall be devoted to your service . . . God
help me to make good my vow, and God bless all of you who
are willing to share in it." At his next public appearance he
venomously mounted the stage to plot regicide.

As part of their ambassadorial service the Oliviers even on
one occasion united the zealous loyalist societies—usually at
one another's throats. They visited Flinders Naval Depot at
Crib Point where Olivier told the sailors—far more interested
in "Viv Leigh than Larry buck"—that he had been a pilot in
the Fleet Air Arm, doing "more damage to the Navy's aircraft
than the Luftwaffe and Der Marine combined". They also flew
to the national capital, Canberra, to take part in the Anzac Day
celebrations, during the course of which they visited the war
memorial, had lunch with the Hon. William McKell, the
Governor-General—very "affable in manner, rather resemb-
ling a Peter Ustinov impersonation". At teatime they met the
Australian Prime Minister, Ben Chifley, and were introduced
to his cabinet. Olivier observed that Chifley was "amiable,
very, if protected by an armour plating of political myster-
ioso".

Having had his patience tested at previous meetings by
questions beginning in such terms as, "Tell us, Sir Laurence,
now that Britain's finished, how will the Empire be divided
up?" Olivier had determined to wade in and seize the opportunity given by such flattering remarks to assert the very
opposite. But feeling apprehensive—he was, after all, merely
an actor—he took Chifley aside and asked him to have a quick
glance through his speech. Chifley's response was to turn his
eyes, "so hooded they were almost shut, away from me . . .
[saying] 'Oh, I would suggest a few impromptu words' . . ."

Olivier ignored Chifley's advice when he spoke that evening to make a Food for Britain appeal at the reunion of the
Returned Servicemen's League in the Capitol Cinema ("really
horrid" with its cramped seating and "Hitlerite mikes"). He
began, "Britain is not finished; she is merely doing what she
has done through history—starting again." And, he went on,
she did not want pity:

If one of your most loving relations in the Mother Country thought for a moment that any of your great kindnesses was provoked by pity, they would hope that not another food parcel, and not even a thought or a sigh, would come from Australia.

He commented later, in the last diary entry, "Arc lights, two movie news cameras, four microphones, six thousand people. Vivien looks wonderful in pale lime green and a blood red rose at her waist. Halfway through she hesitated, but went on, finishing with Sonnet 116." (They borrowed locally a much treasured copy of Shakespeare's *Sonnets* but never returned it—to the owner's dismay.) When they got back to Government House the official secretary told them they had a well-earned rest ahead of them next day. Not at all, they told the secretary, they had a dress rehearsal in the afternoon followed by a heavy first night. Hastily the secretary tried to cover his mistake, "Oh yes, of course, George III" . . . After this Olivier stopped writing his diary.

But while that bright strand in the tour lost none of its apparent lustre, it is hard to conceive of Olivier and Vivien sharing any private life during the Melbourne visit—though perhaps by now the public side of their passion had grown as important, if not more important, than the private side. In May birthdays fell thick and fast—three on 17 May, and on 22 May, a Saturday, Olivier's own forty-first anniversary fell. On 17 May, at the party given for Michael Redington, who was twenty-one, Harold Ingram, and Oliver Hunter, Chico Marx, also appearing at this time in Melbourne, did a send-up of the tango from *The Skin of Our Teeth*. Harold Ingram played two songs from *Oklahoma*, which the Company sang.

After the show on Olivier's birthday the audience sang "Happy Birthday to you", while the owner of the Princess Theatre, Mr Garnet Carroll, invited the whole Company back to his home. They had clubbed together and bought Olivier an antique ashtray, as well as many small individual presents. He had also been given a huge two-tiered cake—devoured during the matinee—followed by two equally enormous cakes at the Carrolls'. Melbourne people also presented Olivier with many gifts. After all this the Oliviers went to bed at 6 am.

Of the continuing drinking and conviviality Elsie remained as disapproving as ever. Even as far back as the end of April, she had received some bad blows to her own vanity. One Saturday her Melbourne hairdresser told her her hair was poor and her style of hairdressing "very old-fashioned". Her morale crumbled. Early in May she declared that "the whole of Melbourne seemed to close in on one and no matter how you hacked away at the work, you just couldn't get through". She attributed much of the fault to the Melbournese (like the blunt hairdresser) and to the place itself, but she also disguised as much as she could another serious cause of her demoralisation: the Oliviers had grown extremely weary of her.

She and Vivien were now openly at loggerheads, Vivien always trying to break out of the motherly restraints she wanted to impose on them as a pair. All too often she (unsuccessfully) treated them as children (they often, remarked Eileen Beldon, reminded one of children—"Flora and Miles in *The Turn of the Screw*"), waiting up for them when they went out after the show, or—when they stayed behind in their hotel—imploring them not to entertain. Herself unmarried and in her middle fifties, Elsie was deeply possessive of Olivier—and therefore jealous of Vivien's hold over him.

Olivier did not know what to do and summoned Charles Wilmot of the British Council to a conference at the Windsor Hotel. Elsie, an efficient administrator in her London base with sometimes as many as seven shows to look after, had never toured before and evidently touring did not put her at her ease. On this particular tour there was increasingly less for her to do, for the Oliviers had Floy Bell, as well as Dan O'Connor and his assistants. In addition also to the British Council (in particular Peter Hiley, who later worked directly for Olivier), there were administrative units in each of the theatres. Therefore Elsie had turned herself into a nursemaid, something of a busybody, and worst of all, a Mrs Grundy.

Yet, paradoxically, because the Company had signed away in their original contracts the right to give interviews—an agreement strictly enforced by the management, with the result that no other actor or actress was, until they relaxed the rule at the end of the Sydney season, interviewed at all—Elsie was often sent along as a substitute for the Oliviers. Therefore she came in for an undue amount of publicity, which usually emerged as of the kind of "Meet the Old Vic 'Mother' ". During most of these interviews she would prattle on about how Sir Laurence and Lady Olivier were two of the kindliest, friendliest people you could ever meet, which must have been far from her thoughts.

When the Oliviers discussed the problem with Charles Wilmot, Vivien was all for sending Elsie home. Short of taking her outside and shooting her, advised the chain-smoking Wilmot, one could not do anything. Olivier, confirming his tendency in that direction, remained too soft-hearted to give her the sack, and Vivien was persuaded that she should be allowed to stay on. From this time on, however, her position in the Company was undermined, and by the end of May she had slipped right out of favour and was seen less and less with Olivier and Vivien. She herself felt "shoved to one side", spending most of the rest of the tour in helping Dan O'Connor, flying off to Hobart, later to Sydney, to fix arrangements for accommodation, and—quite unnecessarily —to inspect facilities in the theatres. The unexpected arrival of the SS *Corinthic* in Melbourne cheered her up, at least temporarily, and gave her an opportunity to renew acquaintanceship with the captain and especially with the purser, Mr Oliver: twelve of the officers saw the show and were entertained to supper after it by the Oliviers.

By now, exceeding their wildest expectations, the Council was making so much money out of the tour that it had started to become an embarrassment. Yet no provision had been made by the Old Vic for any profit. At the end of May Charles Wilmot left in a great hurry for England, while Olivier told Burrell that they were consulting as to what to do for it looked as if all the profit the Old Vic made would stay in Australia to subsidise loss-making musical tours. Olivier's own private arrangements with the Vic ensured that he earned as much, according to one newspaper, as 15 per cent of the gross takings, although the final figure turned out to be less than 3 per cent.

The day before the Melbourne season at the Princess Theatre ended on 12 June Olivier and Vivien attended the

"All I have to offer your daughter, sir, is two tickets for the Olivier show!"

Box offices were working overtime.

première of the film *Hamlet*, whose finished print their agent and close friend Cecil Tennant had brought out to Australia. Happy to have Tennant with them, Olivier made a relaxed and witty speech—"In this fairest of cities there appears to be a little thing called a 'wog' [a throat infection], and I've got it. I can only promise to stay in this theatre for as short a time as possible so that you don't get it, too!"—but the thoughts of Vivien, viewing for the first time Jean Simmons in the part of Ophelia, were far from cheerful. The film, an unqualified success for Olivier, re-awoke for her the pain and bitter memories which had, for nearly six months now, been largely forgotten.

But the Melbourne season itself ended triumphantly. Olivier was bombarded from the stalls with streamers, and he leapt forward to say, "Ladies and gentlemen, our ship hasn't sailed yet!"

3 *Tasmania*

Luckily for them the Oliviers, by leaving later in the day on a different plane, escaped the perilous flight to Hobart. The main body of twenty-six artists took off from Essendon Airport in an old, two-engined Dakota, to fly across the Tasman Sea. When they were well out over the water Georgina Morgan remarked to her husband: "Don't look at the engine. The propeller's going round so fast it isn't going round at all." Said Meg Maxwell: "I thought they were giving it a rest." And there were flames.

Redington, who had just had several teeth filled by a dentist in Melbourne—experiencing for the first time the innovation of cocaine injected into the gum—took a more sanguine view: "I don't know really how bad it was, if I can say now I've been as close to crashing as I ever will without being so, or if it was nothing serious at all."

With jokes such as "Isn't this typical of the Old Vic—so mean they couldn't afford a proper plane", circulating among the Company, the Dakota just managed to reach Western Junction, Launceston, in Northern Tasmania. It missed the runway, where ambulances and fire engines had gathered, and landed in a ploughed field where it did a Christiania ski turn, halted, and stood until a tractor came and towed it back on to the runway. "As the captain left his cabin to walk back to the rear," said Redington, "we all gave him a round of applause."

By now evening had set in: the passengers talked of travelling the last part of the journey by road—a six-hour coach ride around the mountains—but in the end just sat and waited for the engine to be patched up. Pip Barnard and Redington offered to mend the engine but the mechanics said they could manage on their own: in the inadequate glare of torchlight and by using pliers they did their best to fix it, while Barnard and Redington went off and found a billiards table to pass the time. Still on board, the rest of the Company held an Equity meeting and voted not to fly on. However, like most Equity decisions —as someone joked—it was never enforced.

The stay in Hobart was in complete contrast to that in Melbourne. The town was intimate, picturesquely situated in the south of the island, at the foot of Mount Wellington, with a spectacular bay and port. The Theatre Royal, built in 1847 —therefore the oldest theatre in Australia—had unusual charm: tiny, easy on the voice, and providing, compared to what had gone before, a complete holiday. As they were performing one play only, *The School for Scandal*, they could use instead of solid scenery, just the tabs and painted back-cloth. Local stage staff had gone to endless trouble to make the tiny, low-ceilinged dressing rooms ("built by convicts as cells", someone commented, "and impossible to stand up in") comfortable, furnishing them from their own homes, and heating them with a variety of contraptions. But the weather outside was bitterly cold and because the stage had not been used for many years, it still seemed to the actors like a refrigerator. Behind the screen for the famous scene of *School* Vivien installed her mink coat and a little electric fire: Peter Cushing recalled peeping over the top and seeing her perched there on a stool with her latest Simenon.

She and Olivier stayed at the Wrest Point Hotel, which stood on the point of the estuary; on Sunday night they gave their usual press conference which this time they enjoyed immensely. The Tasman press consisted, said a member of the Company, of "very charming and simple people—not at all like the press".

For the opening on Tuesday the audience arrived at the theatre with blankets, and the cast could see their breath freezing in the air. In spite of this the week went extremely

"**Because I believe in practical tributes, that's why.**"

Adverse playing conditions as caricatured by Sprod.

well with, in scaled-down form, the same round of parties and social engagements as before—they met the Governor, the Lord Mayor of Hobart, and visited the University. Olivier again flattered local opinion, this time by telling the people of Hobart that he found their theatre one of the finest he had ever played in; and acoustically its small and perfect scale did act as a tonic to his ailing throat. After one show he made a broadcast in which he passionately advocated the need for more theatres in Australia, and stated, "We do not want the theatre run by the Civil Service."

On 15 June, with more time to themselves than they had had in Melbourne, Olivier and Vivien drove off with Cecil Tennant to visit the interior. Tennant, an ex-Guards officer who towered above both of them—although 5ft 10½in in height Olivier rarely stood up straight—had a cool, aloof, utterly untheatrical manner, and he had accompanied them to Hobart where they found his presence reassuring. For both of them he functioned as a sort of legal guardian. They held on to him as long as they could, even insisting that he should accompany them during the week following the four days in Hobart, on holiday.

Tennant's presence meant, too, they could keep even more clear of Elsie Beyer, though Olivier insisted they take her up to the top of Mount Wellington on 16 June, the date of her fifty-sixth birthday. "It was a beautiful day but again bitterly cold," wrote Elsie, "and you could hardly stand on your feet when you got to the top of the mountain because of the thick snow and ice. However, it was very very nice and one got a wonderful view of the country." One wonders how much she really enjoyed herself. Next day she was packed off to Sydney to try and hunt down a flat for Olivier and Vivien for the forthcoming long season there. Two days later she returned depressed without having found one. News of their problem reached the *Sydney Morning Herald* which reacted sharply, "The Oliviers are having so much trouble getting a residence here, it's rumoured they'll finish up at Admiralty House!"

A large part of the Company stayed in Hobart for their long-awaited break; for them, as for many of the others, this was the high point of the tour. Some travelled back to

Melbourne and some went on to the beaches near Sydney. In Hobart those who had not been staying at Wrest Point moved there to enjoy the fantastic view over the little harbour with Mount Wellington on the left. As Redington described it:

The actual peak was above the clouds, so we saw these waves of clouds and the sun brilliantly shining on us, a lovely sight. But just under the clouds we had this most wonderful view, hills and lakes and we could see for miles and miles, everywhere is so lovely and green, so much like England.

Although defeated in his idea to go skiing in Northern Tasmania Redington, with the Relphs, Eileen Beldon, Peggy Simpson and Hughie Stewart among others, drank black velvet at lunchtime and pure champagne at night. He played tennis at Government House and, in company with the rest, visited all the beauty spots. Fortunately the British Council, in its deliberations as to how to dispose of its huge profit, had decided to be a little more generous towards the Company and give them an entertaining and accommodation allowance, back-dating it to Perth. All had a very lavish week.

Even in the period designated as "holiday", however, the Oliviers were unable to be a very private couple. Vivien, with her tireless social appetite, sought companions, even if her love was reserved for Larry. Dan Cunningham had proved himself useful in this line; Roger Ramsdell had become another member of her entourage, attentive as he was to her creature comforts. Now Cecil Tennant joined the gang and all five set out for a week together, flying to Archerfield, Brisbane, in Queensland. The Oliviers took a suite in a hotel in Surfers' Paradise, Southport. Cunningham rented a bungalow on the shore nearby.

Vivien was finding herself more and more drawn to Cunningham. Like many other young actors and actresses he owed much to Olivier's all-round managerial expertise, and so far had done well on the tour. In *School*, as the pretty rhymster Sir Benjamin Backbite, he gained good notices; in *Richard* his Richmond still grew in stature. Offstage his constant attention to Vivien did not go unnoticed by other members of the Company, in spite of the adage, "Everyone loves Viv." But the love was ritualised. Olivier loved his wife and even the making of love attracted public notice, the stage director, Kentish, reporting in Melbourne that their dressing room door was locked before the curtain rose and Olivier unobtainable because he and Vivien wanted privacy "for an obvious reason". Not a markedly jealous man, Olivier had noticed nothing between Vivien and Cunningham over which he became concerned. Apparently happy that "Puss" could be so harmlessly amused, he could get on with the serious discussions he needed to have with Cecil. But such frivolities were dangerous and only a thin line divided innocence and offence.

While Vivien still burned as his "inspiration", "the guiding light of my life", "the central force of my life, my heart in fact", his frequent diary comments on Vivien's public image lead one to wonder how personal and specific that inspiration now remained. But his more immediate concerns were with forging his Company, testing it—in the tough and constantly differing circumstances provided by Australia—as the nucleus for a National Theatre Company. And by now he felt extremely pleased with the results.

The way the walk-on boys doubled up as dressers, the endless grind undertaken by backstage staff, sometimes working all night setting up scenery and lights: all this instilled a mutual loyalty which never died (many years later Bill Bundy, for example, joined him in the first National Theatre Company). In particular David Kentish always spread a terrific ray of efficiency which, said Olivier, "fairly blinded the diggers" but likewise his personal staff and the wardrobe.

The actors more than surpassed his expectations too, and effusive though he could be socially he was most fastidious and forceful in praise and criticism of actors, bestowing them carefully and only seldom making appreciative comment which, when it came, seemed reward enough for effort. As Margaret Leighton once said, "He never praises you professionally unless he really means it . . . he can be ruthless or tough but always in the interests of his craft." In particular, he judged Mercia Swinburne had improved beyond what he had thought possible. Eileen Beldon and he had, since they had first acted together in the 1920s in Birmingham, always had a

difficult relationship and he commented that she seemed
impossible to coordinate. Bernard Merefield he found to be a
bit of a worry and though Merefield tried his damnedest
Olivier felt he no longer had the necessary strength and
vitality. But Vivien, he thought, had made great strides
forward in technique. All this, as a good commanding officer,
he noted well. But in that maelstrom it was, as he told Cecil,
impossible to find time really to concentrate or to read anything new.

Unknown to him, and far from restoring their relationship
as he had hoped, four months of being together day and night
had made Vivien lose confidence in him. At one level—and on
his own terms—he made contact easily: he clowned, he led, he
cajoled, he never spared himself. In their early days together he
had given of himself easily, he had been vulnerable, he had
been close to her. Now, in some yet undefined way, he had
withdrawn. While he remained as inwardly vulnerable as ever,
his knighthood, his sense of leadership made him expect so
much more of himself. He told Helen Cushing how lonely in
his position he had become because no one had the temerity to
tell him how his performances stood up to so much repetition.

Vivien had been against his accepting the knighthood.
When he had been unreasonably jealous of Ralph Richardson
receiving a knighthood before him, she had consoled him with
her conviction that artists should not be rewarded by the state,
for it placed them in a false and compromised position. Their
own irreverent spirit—combined with their natural regality as
a pair—made such an artificial honour look ridiculous. After
he had accepted it she still insisted on being known as Vivien
Leigh. Now with horror she saw that, even though he joked
about it, his knighthood had become sacred to him.

Of course she knew his love for her was still a religion to
him, but recognised that as it had in its outer observance of
ritual grown, so its inner content had waned. Also he did not
seem to understand—perhaps never would—the difference
between loving someone (enjoyably secure in your own feeling), and transforming that feeling into a form of expression
relative to the loved one's need.

Richard III had much to do with this changed feeling she
noticed in him. Not that he acted all the time (as his third wife,

Joan Plowright, later observed)—far from it. He had developed the capacity of being able to step out of character and
turn to other things. During performances of *Richard*—while
members of the Company gave him a wide berth—he would,
during the interval, call in Floy Bell and dictate letters.

But ruthlessly applied ambition now held, Vivien saw, a
fascination for Olivier which he never quite shrugged off
again. Others had at this time noticed it: Ralph Richardson, his
oldest friend and adviser, had felt it taking over: Olivier now
had to be first in every race. On each occasion that he played
Richard he revised and reinforced that inner heartlessness. It
shocked Vivien and some nights she noticed there was something almost obscene about the performance's naked revelation of power. Did Larry love Richard too much? That last
electrifying twenty minutes took everything out of him. It
stood as an act of love greater than any he ever made to
her—and it took place in public. Richard's death throes were
—there could be no other description—a most remarkable
orgasm, and as such the symbol of his total commitment. She
longed for him to return to Chekhov and play Astrov again:
this would always be her favourite part of his. But at this time
Olivier rejected the tubercular sensitivity, the understanding
and pathos of Chekhov: when things got bad, when problems
threatened to shake his attachment to his work, he would with
a grim joke shut himself off from them. The born adventurer
who captured the imagination by boldness, he would let
impulse and intuition, not premeditation, control his actions:

> I have set my life upon a cast
> And I will stand the hazard of the die.

In another, darker mood she must have told herself that
their love was doomed. For what, otherwise, could have made
it so fascinating to others? Over the crowds that mobbed them
hovered an element of unreality: the hundreds of women
waiting to touch her, or to maul him, were an expression of
hysterical fantasy which found recognition inside her. Public
celebration of love could easily turn into public sacrifice. She
sensed this more than Olivier who saw the crowd more than
anything else as a collection of extras which boosted his

confidence: like Coriolanus he could reveal his scars to the people only the better to place his boot upon their necks.

To hide her vulnerability she split the crowd into individuals with separate names and identities. But they still looked at her, assessing her, measuring themselves against her—watching and waiting to see when she would crack. Even when she and Olivier left for Queensland on holiday, neither the reporters nor the crowd at Mascot Airport, Sydney, would leave them alone. Larry had to explain: "We are entitled to some privacy. When we are on the job we put everything we have into it, and we want to relax completely now."

Flat in mood after months of excitement and exposure, Vivien blamed part of Larry's withdrawal on herself. She knew the shortcomings of her nature: "My birth sign is Scorpio and they eat themselves up and burn themselves out," she later told the reporter David Lewin. She knew Scorpio to be the strongest and most extreme sign of all, especially in sex, and that intensity of feeling—above all a need for its reciprocation—were cardinal characteristics of her nature. Scorpios had complex moods, and when they loved they loved deeply: but they were notorious for wearing out their partners. They played for too high stakes, and would only ever be rewarded with extremes: extreme success, extreme failure, extreme love, extreme lack of love.

At first they had wanted to holiday on the Great Barrier Reef: again an extreme notion of Vivien's which Cecil quashed, saying, "How often have you been to Moscow for a few days' rest?" Instead they had booked in at the Surfers' Paradise Hotel, but the press found out and five hundred people surrounded them at Archerfield Airdrome as soon as they landed. At the hotel it turned out to be far worse: hundreds of people cheered nervously, following them and stretching out autograph books wherever they went. The prurient would crane their necks or climb on balconies to peer into their bedroom, mob them in the streets, ogle them as they stretched out on the beach. They had no idea Surfers' Paradise was so popular. Olivier donned a white panama and dark glasses; Vivien hid in their room, still recuperating from bronchitis, and wailing incessantly of her desire to return to

Tasmania. After one night they disappeared, driving in secret along the coast to Broadbeach where Cunningham had his bungalow. Here they spent what time there was left.

The few days' holiday revitalised Olivier. He could bounce back amazingly quickly, resisting fate just as he could resist the crowd, flinging its call for gladiatorial blood, its lust for disaster, back in its own face. He always had work to do. His talent, like an element in nature, was explosive and self-renewing, incorporating, above all, the power of lightning, striking unexpectedly, creating fear and revelation: "The power of a ruler," runs an old Chinese text, "is like the lightning flash, though its force is less."

But the conflict remained inside Vivien, and Olivier could no longer provide the stability to counter it. He began to notice the change in her though neither of them owned up to any weakening of faith.

PART THREE

The Society of Mammals

Australia and America are at the old racket and they'll pay the old price. And one's already seen everything that was Europe's best shat on, parodied.

Sidney Nolan

1   Sydney

Originally their plan had been to open in Sydney on Tuesday 22 June but because of the holiday, the first night was delayed until a week later. As the sets for *School* had been duplicated for Hobart, and as they had closed in Melbourne with *The Skin of Our Teeth*, the full-scale Cecil Beaton scenery had already arrived in Sydney and been unpacked. *The School for Scandal* had now been performed more times than the other two plays and while in relation to them the acting had improved, the costumes were showing wear and tear, so the wardrobe people had much maintenance and renovation to carry out. *School* had easily become the Company's own favourite.

To the horror of Olivier and the rest, the Tivoli Theatre in Sydney was only slightly less large than the Capitol, Perth. Yet fortunately, unlike the Capitol, it had not been designed primarily as a cinema, and the acoustics were far superior. Here they had eight shows a week including two matinées, the total adding up to, for *School*, twenty-five, for *Richard*, seventeen, and for *Skin*, eighteen performances. Since Vivien had the leading role in *Skin*, Olivier in *Richard*, and they shared the largest roles in *School*, in Sydney each was to give sixty performances and expected to be seen by nearly 120,000 people.

None of the Company complained that the Oliviers had too big a slice of the parts or attention (and a small but substantial percentage of the tour's overall profit). Because they led from the front, thinking more of those they commanded than of themselves, quite the reverse was felt: as Peter Cushing said, "Such was their attitude to all of us throughout that remarkable tour. *We* came *first*." Unconscious flattery of others had always been a key constituent of Olivier's enormous magnetism. A Sydney man who visited backstage one night after a performance asked a stage-hand if the Oliviers had left, to be told, "Oh no, they haven't come and said goodnight, and they'd never leave without doing that."

The Company had split into smaller groups or cliques who went around together, but among them—or among the married couples—there was no quarrelling. No wild or excessive behaviour, or even malicious gossip, marred the tour. Again Cushing put his finger on the cohesive quality: "There was no drawing aside of screens, it had become a real unit." Only Mum and Dad "in loco" fell out, not knowing if they loved each other any more, but like proud, old-fashioned parents, kept it from the children and presented to them a devoted and united front.

But if by now it had become a model family was it, as Olivier hoped, a prototype National Theatre Company, or was it, as some of the Governors of the Old Vic increasingly hinted at or whispered, a very old-fashioned actors' touring company run by an autocratic actor-manager and his wife as a kind of personal fiefdom?

Olivier was sure in his own mind that it was the former: when he first joined the Old Vic he had bound himself to a twelve-year plan, believing he was building himself the right to a permanent job, and hoping, as he put it, that his influence would help to "leaven the sepulchral destiny inevitably associated with such institutions". From this had been generated his extraordinary commitment to the tour: to prove the validity of such a company, and his own ability to lead it, and to deal with all the company's artistic, political and public relations aspects that might be involved. What could be more directly in the line of duty of a National Theatre after a world war than to be leading a triumphantly successful tour of the Dominions?

In the cramped Hobart dressing room, after one performance of *School*, Olivier had now, at last, made a long broadcast for ABC, returning to the theme of previous speeches in Adelaide and Melbourne, of a National Theatre for Australia. He believed in the value of theatre as a whole, he repeated in that slightly unfortunate phrase, as the "glamouriser of thought". "We all remember our young days in the theatre," he continued in his rambling, but vivid and extempore fashion, with its mixture of the clerical and the Shakespearean ("Wouldn't it be nice," he once said, "if everybody were a trifle Shakespearean?"). The theatre must be kept up, and kept alive; if Australia had a National Theatre, "*there* would be the body with the heart beating in it". He was to return to play more variations on this theme while in Sydney.

"My God he does look well after his holiday," wrote Redington, "and so much energy, he re-produced *School* this afternoon!" The rest of the Company arrived variously by plane, train and coach, finding Sydney very different from the other towns. "I like it very much," said Redington. "It is funny the way people say we will not like it at all . . . Everyone said it moved too quickly and you could not find your way about: it is rather hard at first, I must admit . . . the shops are excellent, and there's one really super one called David Jones, where they sell 'lovely English material at half the price you would have to pay for it in England'."

Practically all the Company found accommodation in bed-sits with cooking facilities in a block in the King's Cross area of Sydney, and settled down well, although worried that because the Government had started to ration gas and electricity they would be caught using these at not those hours which had been prescribed by law.

Only on the Friday before arrival had Elsie Beyer procured for the Oliviers a flat in Cremorne, a Sydney suburb. Olivier and Vivien drove out in their hired Humber to see it, unpacked their luggage and settled in for the night. "It's a very nice flat," piped up Elsie to the press, but a few mornings later the Oliviers moved into the Hotel Australia. One Cremorne neighbour remarked: "How could you expect them to stay in a flat where they have no heating, no hot water, and no facilities to cook meals late at night after the show?"

At the Hotel Australia restrictions also applied—no switching on of central heating and a limit of two lights' use in each suite. But they could get hot water and meals at all hours. Elsie consoled herself, "The flat was a little far out": it seemed that she had failed them in the sole function left to her. "It's across a big bridge, but I don't suppose I'll ever know where it is as I travel to and fro by car," was Vivien's tossed-off description: "but it has a beautiful view of the water."

On the first Monday in Sydney, after the refreshing holiday and with morale again high, the Oliviers attended a press reception at Usher's Hotel: Vivien ("she looked like a bit of gossamer"; she "makes you think of a lovely pearl") enlivened this by declaring that she was taking back to England a Jerboa rat, which "hops like a kangaroo", to give as a pet to Ralph Richardson. Asked if she had considered a platypus, she answered no because they cost about "£40 a week in worms". But she was also buying gum trees and tree ferns for Notley. She loved, she went on, "your kookaburras. Isn't it fun the way all the little ones sit on a limb, huddled so close together that they keep pushing the end one off? And the parents sit below in a disinterested way."

"I once thought I'd like to be Sir Laurence Olivier," wrote the reporter of the *Sydney Morning Herald*,

> but not after the time the press boys and press girls gave him at Usher's last night: they did everything but play football with him.
>
> They knew they had the best of him once they got him in the corner.
>
> I don't know whether someone pushed Sir Laurence, but he sat down on the lowest couch I've ever seen.
>
> The rest was easy.
>
> The questions fired at him! They covered just about everything in the encyclopaedia. And he smiled through the whole performance.
>
> Just when we'd reached some high cultural plane one fellow at the back yelled: "Break it up; let's have a go at him!"

After the reception had finished, at 8.45 pm, Olivier held a lighting rehearsal until 2 am.

School opened to a smart and distinguished audience, which included the Governor-General (The Hon W. J. McKell) and many other notables, five of whom wore silk top hats. Some rare bird life festooned the house: one woman had three tiny white humming birds, complete in every detail, pinned across the back of her head; another carried as a cap two whole birds of vivid pink and blue.

After the final curtain and an enthusiastic response of six calls, Olivier made his usual unprepared speech: "We have been a long time coming here, but tonight has been a joy to us all. We thank you deeply for your wonderful reception. We feel this play could be better perpetrated, but it could never be more nobly received." Again, said the critics, he had demonstrated his two-fold stature—as actor and as director—combining, as the critic of the *Daily Telegraph* wrote, the "formalism of the eighteenth century with the fluid technique of the film". The same critic found Vivien as Lady Teazle enchanting—"her beauty was in exquisite contrast to the teasing and vexatious young lady of fashion she portrayed" —and liked especially Peter Cushing as Joseph Surface, and Eileen Beldon's "monstrous and monumental" Mrs Candour.

But the same post-holiday zest did not transform or renew *Richard*, and its first night, Friday 2 July, evoked a more restrained enthusiasm from press and public. This time, though plentifully supplied with fur coats, the crowd wore more subdued colours, and while critics praised the central performance and main thrust of the action, including in their praise Peter Cushing's Clarence and George Relph's Buckingham, they gave little cheer to the rest of the Company (beyond politely remarking upon Vivien's beauty). For instance Josephine O'Neill commented, "Even within the limitations of the play, which subordinated all roles to that of Richard, the Old Vic Company displayed marked weakness." Her remarks were echoed a few weeks later by Olivier writing to John Burrell: "*Richard* is in a perfectly shocking state, and I have taken the curse off it by some extremely colourful lighting effects which may not be to your taste but something had to be done as it is literally falling apart and looks like it."

Then it happened. At the second performance of *Richard*, a Saturday matinée, Olivier flung himself into that astounding display of stage craft, doubling up and unleashing himself against Dan Cunningham's noble Richmond—who as usual recoiled somewhat—then slipped, injuring his right knee. He fell in agony.

After the matinée rumour spread that Olivier had broken his leg. This was not the case. He had torn a cartilage in the knee, claiming later that his limp in Richard, in constantly fatigued conditions, had set up a weakness in the "straight" leg. As it was Saturday the whole of Macquarie Street, where many doctors and specialists had practices, had closed down, and Elsie, at last with a full-scale emergency to respond to, contacted the hospital. Two doctors, one a leading orthopaedic surgeon, examined Olivier in his dressing room, bandaged the knee, and gave him a shot of morphine for the pain. But he suffered mental distress also, asking himself why in troubled times one's body felt called upon to jump on the bandwagon. However, and though still in great pain, he got through the evening performance: the fight was cut, so were the death throes. He would—as has often been pointed out—die rather than miss a performance.

At the hospital on Sunday morning he had an x-ray which did not reveal any bone damage. The doctors told him to rest the knee and it would right itself, and while he enjoyed making his pedantic joke that he had "damaged the anterior median horn of the meniscus", his mind was already working furiously to resolve what to do in future performances of the plays. In *Richard III* he first thought of reversing his costume in order to drag his injured right leg, but this presented many problems. Next day he found a period crutch which he put to brilliant use, integrating it into his performance just as if Shakespeare had written the part for an actor using a crutch. So expert did he become in its employment that on Monday night he broke it in rage on the back of George Cooper, playing Brackenbury, and stage-hands had to work frantically to make it a new end. He gestured with it so effectively that it came to epitomise, in its stumpy thrusts, the naked and lustful power-seeking of Richard. It even revitalised, by the constraint and challenge it imposed on his performance—together with the tension and awe it awoke in the rest of the cast—the whole role. If there was, as the *Sydney Bulletin* (on 7 July) insisted, a "crack right across it" (meaning the production) Olivier's period crutch sealed that crack. Henceforth all could only register amazement at Olivier's guts. The crutch made such a hit that not only was it featured in a political cartoon, it also became fashionable among "young bloods" to sport a stick—even though they had nothing wrong with their legs.

But then, hard on *Richard III* in that second gruelling week, came *The Skin of Our Teeth*.

By now lots of Old Vic jokes were in circulation in Sydney.

THE DAILY MIRROR, WEDNESDAY, JULY 7, 1948.

OPEN THE DOOR, RICHARD!

"My dear, the things they're saying about *The Skin of Our Teeth*! There hasn't been so much chatter in the salons and the saloons since Sweeney Todd, the Demon Barber." One man described it as "Hellzapoppin without Olsen and Johnson". "Though Oscar was Wilde, Thornton was Wilder" showed the general level of newspaper wit. One comment ran, "We understand that Sir Laurence Olivier will NOT be giving a lecture to the Dental Association on 'The Skin of our Teeth'." (About the only address, Olivier must have reflected, he did not give.)

As for audiences, the *Tribune* claimed under the headline "A Play for Morons and Lunatics", they scratched their heads and did as they were told. Yet if anything *Skin*, looking forward as it did to the Theatre of the Absurd, proved ahead of its time, and as a whole the highly individualistic Sydney people found it less puzzling than expected, minding less than Melbourne the sophistication and zaniness—perhaps because they had been forewarned.

One critic called it a "startling and gusty [*sic*] mixture of vaudeville, pantomime, serious drama and old morality plays"; another related how it told the history of mankind in the "rip-roaring temper of a cheap-street music hall where patrons, if so moved, may whistle and boo and throw up their hats until Vivien Leigh at long last emerges in her 1905 bathing suit". The word "surrealism" cropped up several times, while someone else pointed out that *Skin* was nearer in style to the Tivoli "low-brow" tradition, though none of the Tivoli "lovelies" came anywhere near Vivien Leigh, especially in the second act "when as a beauty contest winner she flaunts her allure among the male members of the Society of Mammals" —a marvellous example of unconscious double-meaning.

One member of the audience wrote that he and his party had seats in a back row near the stairs where just before the interval the boys with soft drinks gathered behind them. Act Two ended dramatically with the Deluge. "It must have been a bit too exciting for one boy as at that very moment we experienced the deluge literally, as he tipped his tray of drinks over our backs." Another declared, "I do not think we really understood *The Skin of Our Teeth* but the sight of Scarlett O'Hara on stage was really something." But Vivien became distraught at the lack of audience response, hinting in an interview that "bewilderment was evident in its coldness".

At her urging, Olivier at the next performance made a highly unusual pre-curtain speech encouraging the spectators to laugh and not be frightened of applauding. Starved of live theatre Australian audiences had, he said, lost the knack of being audiences. His direct method worked and the response got better.

In *Skin* Olivier again turned his injury to advantage. Returning as the weary hero from the Napoleonic Wars, Antrobus hears Mrs Antrobus ask him, "Are you still limping, dear?" and replies, "My wounds are still troubling me from that other battle." Olivier made sure the audience caught the reference to Bosworth. In other scenes he adapted his gait ingeniously, trudging about painfully as the weary workman, later swinging a cane that enhanced his silk hat, striped pants and tail coat.

In Sydney it emerged that Australians loved joking about their ignorance, to give the idea that culture was a bit over their heads. The discomfiting story caught on of a woman who came backstage just after a performance of *Richard III* to tell Olivier, "You weren't *bad* tonight. A bit shaky at first, but you warmed up to the part later on. Did you ever know an actress called Imogene Wise? Now there was someone who *really* knew her Shakespeare." Another mischievous tale had, during the interval of *Richard*, a "stallite" declaring, "It's all right, you know, I liked Lady Leigh, but when does Olivier come on?"

The most deflationary piece of all featured a "punchbowl red-head" who allocated tickets for the Tivoli (many thousands of applications were turned down): "After reading so many hysterical letters from women wanting to get a good look at [Olivier] I feel quite apathetic about him," she said. She claimed that from her job she had discovered that the average human being was not very bright. For example, one person requested, "If you can't get me seats for *Hamlet* or any of the other operas, could you send me a seat for the Town Hall concerts." What had that got to do with the Old Vic? she asked. Someone else wrote that he needed good seats because he was "crippled, part deaf and very unhappy". A third, that he was "much too fat to fit comfortably in a gallery seat and . . . could we find him a nice comfy spot in the lounge?"

If Olivier had once thought Australia could provide him and Vivien with the opportunity to recoup something lost in their relationship he must, by the end of the second week in Sydney, have realised how badly mistaken he was. The journalistic emphasis placed on the pair indicated how different Sydney was from Perth and Adelaide; Sydney being no starry-eyed backwater but a wealthy and magnificent city, it thought, like Alexander Korda, of the Oliviers' love story in terms of money and commercial exploitation. At various cinemas a short time after their arrival there were no less than five films running in which one or other, or both, appeared—*Lady Hamilton, Waterloo Bridge, Henry V, Pride and Prejudice, Rebecca*. In addition to these *Hamlet* was due to open at the end of July, while the Old Vic season was expected to make over £A100,000 (finally £A120,000 had to be returned to unsuccessful applicants for seats). As Olivier later pointed out, "Sydney not only claimed to be as sophisticated a city as could be found in the civilised world, but wished one to be aware that if it was influenced by anyone it was by America rather than Britain, and so indeed it seemed." He might have been echoing a visiting journalist who wrote that Sydney was cruder than Chicago, more violent than New York, more beautiful than San Francisco, and money mad. As a city which looked to the future, Sydney was the harbinger of a more materialistic age when chivalric love would be dead.

Did Australians have a real appetite for drama, or were they, by their support of the tour, just reaching for status? The climax of the Old Vic Company's visit had now been reached and, as if to underline this, in Sydney it was arranged that all three plays be recorded for radio and transmitted over the whole sub-continent. Although in odd instances people had travelled up to two thousand miles to see the Company perform, so far its ports of call had only covered a small percentage of the population: country dwellers had had virtually no chance to see them. The magic wireless would rectify this.

In a leader earlier that year the *Morning Herald* had made it clear how substantially Sydney's theatre had declined from the time, not so long before, of eight or nine continuously occupied theatres. One of the main reasons had been films. But lack of competition had played an equally important part, for a whole generation had grown up hardly witnessing any live theatre. Given that already bad situation, the *Herald* went on, Actors' Equity had made it worse by treating theatrical artists as if they were tradesmen and by imposing rigorous quotas on visiting artists. (Fortunately and so far the unions had not intervened in the Old Vic's affairs though disputes here and there had caused a little trouble, notably in Perth over whether or not scenery was an "import", and in Melbourne over the employment of a few extra walk-ons.) Olivier's presence lent support to those wanting to reverse the decline:

There is a tremendous craving for the theatre in this country, yet from what I can gather the only permanent theatre companies of local origin are the companies at the Minerva Theatre and Doris Fitton's Independent Theatre. One thing needed is a theatre school, where young players can be trained. Another thing—and I am very emphatic about this—is the freest exchange of British and Australian artists. The formation of a National Theatre is not the first step by any means. That may come later. A National Theatre will give you fine buildings, but not actors and actresses.

So great an effect did these and similar utterances have, that Olivier was invited, during their stay in Sydney, to pick a site for a national theatre, though sensibly he declined.

Emotional impetus apart Olivier and the Company also had a lasting effect on the mechanics of play production in Australia. Before they came there had always been long intervals —even between scenes—during which elaborate sets .were switched around—with noisy banging and voices heard behind the curtain. "The Olivier Productions", according to Beryl Graham, an Education Officer at the Australian Museum, Sydney, "first showed here that the simplest reversal of some part of the scenery, or silent addition of a potted tree, or lantern, or whatever it was, could create the appropriate atmosphere."

The ambassadorial effect of the tour also held strong in Sydney, with all members of the Company now feeling, in a rather bizarre way, that when local people got up to toast the King they had to fill in as the King's representatives and say thank you on his behalf. With the break-up of a large part of the Empire imminent, Australians wanted to demonstrate loyalty—Olivier, to his intense embarrassment, found himself for the second time taking the salute at a naval march past. Vivien had to address official wives' associations and attend garden parties and fashion shows at which she flew the flag for English houses like Hardy Amies. Both visited hospitals and attended university functions. Even the very youngest members of the Company, at schools or other places to which they had been invited, found themselves expected to lecture on Shakespeare or on acting. As the wartime ethos of survival through improvisation had stuck with most of them, they generally carried out such extra duties superbly. Here, again, Olivier's leadership gave them heart.

Their Sydney hosts, too, insisted they share what theatre they did have with their guests. Michael Redington discovered by such means,

> an excellent play,* all about a group of Australian soldiers in the very north of Australia. It was a play that could only be done by Australians and only appreciated by Australians. I think though, that if an all-Australian cast did bring it to England it would go down very well, because the theme of it, boredom of war, can be appreciated by hundreds of people. The only trouble about it is the swearing, every minute they said "bastard", or "Christ" and "Jesus". You know that "bastard" is the greatest term of endearment out here.

Olivier was only too aware that in Melbourne he had been off four nights ("with an acute attack of the laryngeal chords of the pharynx") and Vivien off seven, so—except for Olivier's accident—in Sydney they took greater care of themselves in order to get through the long season. But they kept up the popular practice of birthday parties for members of the Company.

One Sunday in early July they organized an outing for the May-June-July people, among them Peter Cushing: a passionate collector of model soldiers, he received from the Oliviers a whole set of boy scouts complete with flags. They drove in two coaches to Whale Beach, forty miles from Sydney; here at Jonah's Restaurant, on a hill overlooking the sea and the bay, with the sun shining directly down on them, they had a barbecue and ate chops and sausages, and drank pint after pint. Afterwards the party staggered down on to the beach, where in order to get Olivier near the sea so that he could swim, two

---

* *Rusty Bugles* by Sumner Locke-Elliott: according to Leslie Rees in *The Making of Australian Drama* this opened at Doris Fitton's North Sydney Independent Theatre on 21 October—Redington attended a public read-through before that date. *Rusty Bugles* broke all box-office records and enabled its author to achieve his ambition—domicile in the US.

of them made with their arms a "cat's cradle" and carried him
down. Once there, he and several others who had been
foolhardy enough to bring their "bathers" plunged into the
water, much to the amazement of the locals (in Sydney it was
still mid-winter).

"I think they found it rather cold, but wouldn't admit to it,"
commented Elsie. "David Kentish's tummy was something to
be seen, he had eaten seven chops and five sausages, the
record," observed Redington. Then everyone played tip
and run and had great fun (a "very peculiar cricket match",
Elsie called it). As a result of this beach party they decided to
form a cricket team, and challenge the Tivoli stage staff to a
game.

On Thursday 15 July Elsie glumly logged her state: "Nothing much to report today except that I retired to my bed as I
had a bad throat and thought it best to keep it to myself." That
day, unremarked on by the General Manager, already had
become, in fact, the most momentous of the tour, for on 9 July
Lord Esher, Chairman of the Old Vic Governors, wrote
Olivier a letter enclosing what he termed a private and con-
fidential Memorandum of future Administration at the Old
Vic: the Memorandum explained itself, and there would be
plenty of time, he said, for Olivier to discuss it on his return,
while its ultimate success depended upon the proposed
appointments. His letter concluded with fulsome praise:

> I cannot close without sending to you the appreciation of the
> Governors for the great work, not only for England but for
> the reputation of the Old Vic, that you and the Company
> have accomplished in the Dominions. We fully realize the
> sacrifice that you have made and the increasing and exhaust-
> ing work that the great position you have made for yourself
> entails. It will remain an outstanding landmark in your
> distinguished career.

The document was a bombshell: in effect what it said was
that the Old Vic should begin to expand into its role as a
National Theatre and needed a different command structure:
so it proposed dismantling the directors-in-triplicate of Olivier, Richardson, and Burrell in favour of a permanent ad-

ministrator who was "not to act save in very exceptional circumstances". For the three directors this meant the sack.

The document had also been sent to Richardson in Hollywood, to Burrell in London, but it took the longest time to reach Olivier in Sydney, arriving there the same day as a cable from Burrell:

LAURENCE OLIVIER   TIVOLI THEATRE
SYDNEY   AUSTRALIA

DEAR LARRY ESHER HAS SENT ME
GOVERNORS MEMORANDUM ON
REORGANISATION AND COPY HIS LETTER TO
YOU stop WISH TO STRESS THIS PREPARED IN
CAMERA WITHOUT MY KNOWLEDGE stop
HAVE REPLIED ESHER PROTESTING AT ONE
OUR NOT BEING CONFIDED IN TWO
PREPARATION AND CIRCULATION OF
MEMORANDUM DURING YOUR AND RALPHS
ABSENCE AND THREE REQUESTING NO
FURTHER STEPS TILL YOU BOTH RETURN
WHEN ALL SEVEN DIRECTORS AVAILABLE FOR
DISCUSSIONS stop MICHEL GEORGE GLEN
HUGH★ ALL VERY ANNOYED AND MAKING
DIGNIFIED PROTESTS stop PLEASE DO NOT
REPLY ESHER UNTIL YOU GET MY LETTER
AND COPY MY LETTER TO HIM AIRMAILED
TODAY SINCE IMPORTANT WE REACT IN
UNITED WAY AND AVOID ATTEMPTS DRIVE
WEDGES BETWEEN US WHILE SEPARATED stop
MIGHT BE PREFERABLE SEND YOUR
REACTIONS TO ME FOR TRANSMISSION ESHER
stop AM SENDING IDENTICAL CABLE RALPH
stop HAS ANTIGONE ARRIVED AND IS KNEE
BETTER MUCH LOVE JOHN

Olivier had begun to dread playing Richard, especially the double-dose on matinée days. Thursday 15 July was such a

---

★ Michel Saint-Denis, George Devine, Glen Byam Shaw, Hugh Hunt.

day. Receiving Esher's letter, couched, as Olivier said, "in the brightest jolliest terms", was "so ironical that I was hysterical with laughter. For heaven's sake! Here I was, fourteen thousand miles away from home, right in the middle of building up a splendid new company for the Old Vic. It was so incredible a surprise that, as in a farce, laughter was a reflex action."

Bitterly, he kept the news to himself, confiding only in Vivien, and for the present making no reply.

Tyrone Guthrie and the Old Vic governors had originally requested Olivier, Burrell and Richardson to run the Old Vic Company until a year after the war ended. Before the expiry of that agreement they had extended the run of the directors-in-triplicate to five years while they expanded their responsibilities to include all Old Vic drama activities. In particular they had developed a twelve-year plan for a National Theatre tie-up with the Old Vic. The governors and directors also initiated the Old Vic School which in time deeply influenced the British theatre. (On the tour, Thomas Heathcote had been appointed its representative, and he and Elsie had already held auditions for Australian applicants and awarded one or two studentships.)

To develop a second Company was also part of the long-term plan and therefore the governors had agreed to the tour, but the choice of plays had been criticised by at least two members of the board, one of them being Tyrone Guthrie who had already disagreed violently with Olivier over the inspired notion of combining *Oedipus* and *The Critic* in a double bill at the New Theatre, and who now claimed that *Richard III* was too much of a star vehicle and *The Skin of Our Teeth* too frivolous. Increasingly, Guthrie had let it be known that he objected to an Old Vic run by a pair of actor-manager knights. But in 1947 and 1948 the governors had agreed to Richardson catching up on several film offers and Richardson remained absent from London; the governors also released Olivier in 1947 for his film of *Hamlet*. Before 1948 the more hard-boiled and commercially minded Bronson Albery had let it be known in emphatic terms that he viewed the forthcoming absences of Richardson and Olivier with grave misgivings.

During this period Lord Lytton, Chairman of the Board of

Governors, who had been sympathetic towards the triumvirate, had died and his ultimate replacement—his immediate successor, Lord Hambleden, had also been rapidly struck down—the icy and ambitious Viscount Esher, now sixty-seven, became, though for different reasons, an ally of Guthrie's. Esher's long-term aim was also for the Old Vic to be the seedbed for a National Theatre, but to head this he had in mind others than actors of the calibre of Olivier and Richardson. Another influential governor, Barbara Ward (later Baroness Jackson of Lodsworth), also held the belief that the director of a National Theatre should not be an actor.*

During the autumn prior to Olivier's departure on the Antipodean tour there had been a rising sense of crisis, and in the spring of 1948 little could disguise the fact that in the absence of Olivier and Richardson the London Company had passed through a bad winter. A whispering campaign began, the detractors of the Company exaggerating its decline, deceiving those who would listen over the absence of its two leading players, and over the extent to which the Company had become a two-star (some went so far as to say one-star) vehicle. These same detractors now gloated over the feed-back of the ecstatic Australian press which lauded "Sir Laurence Olivier's Old Vic Company." "Whose Old Vic?" they would ask in superior fashion. Olivier might, wrote their leading apologist Charles Landstone, "have reflected on the tragedy of Richard I, and remembered what happened to the kingdom of the Lion Heart, when that monarch was on his wanderings".

Lord Esher, who had been in charge of the planning committee, now succeeded Lord Hambleden, who died in March. "I am sorry for every one of the participants in the Old Vic tragedy," further wrote Landstone. "They have been the shuttlecocks of fate." Amid the plotting and counter-plotting one crucial faction against the triumvirate stood out: the committee set up in 1947 to amalgamate at some future time

---

* Later Lord Chandos, formerly Oliver Lyttelton, Chairman of the Governors of the National Theatre, of which Olivier was appointed first director in 1962, thought that to have an actor as first director of the National Theatre was "perhaps an organisational mistake. But nevertheless it is what has brought the National Theatre off the ground, entirely due to Larry."

the Old Vic with a National Theatre, a scheme over which Lord Lytton presided until his death. Oliver Lyttelton, another key member of the Board, was enthusiastic over this new Committee, calling it "a contract of marriage pending the consummation of the marriage", and Esher now managed to persuade Sir Stafford Cripps—one of Ben Chifley's heroes —to earmark £1 million of Treasury funds towards building a theatre. Olivier had always been one hundred per cent behind the scheme. He knew that his detractors were helped at this stage by the fact that the 1947–8 season had made a small loss (though towards the end business had been picking up) for the first time, and so necessitating an increase in the possible subsidy—the budgets had been underwritten but no use had up to then been made of the guaranteed sums. In this connection Olivier had felt frustrated they could not make use of the profits building up in Australia from the tour, writing to Burrell from Melbourne, "I rather wish the dear Vic had a larger slice of the takings, as it might help matters a bit—no? V. worrying the returns have been lately, haven't they? I have a feeling that maybe, poor boy, there is a difficult time going on for you with the Govs and people like that, and that future plans have been harder than usual to get into order."

Only too true, but neither Olivier nor Burrell knew how carefully the case had been prepared against all three of them, and the many exaggerated arguments which had been put forward—one claim made was that without Olivier the Company could do no good work. Tyrone Guthrie described Olivier and Richardson as trying to have the cake and eat it. Both he and the others saw their opportunity while both men were away and unable at short notice to return. Their very lack of response would be interpreted as showing their want of commitment. Someone quoted from Ibsen's *The Pretenders*: "Norway has been a kingdom. It must become a people."

After an appalling weekend of gales, rain and low temperatures, Olivier at last received the promised letter from John Burrell in which he said how disappointed he felt not to have been allowed to visit Larry in Australia. Esher had been taking a very irritable line, while George Chamberlain, another member of the board, had made a vehement speech claiming Burrell would be worn out by the air trip. Burrell also pointed out the impracticality of Esher's plan; he wrote that one does not like to be suspicious, but it was blatantly ridiculous, surely, with the completion of the National Theatre at least ten years away, for the governors to be tackling this question now. On receiving Burrell's letter Olivier, having by now begun to form plans for a rival company though keeping them up his sleeve, cabled him with an interim response:

DEAR JOHNNIE ESHER LETTER AND MEMORANDUM RECEIVED WHICH SHALL ACKNOWLEDGE BY LETTER stop HAVE ASKED CECIL APPROACH YOU FOR PRIVATE INFORMATION stop WOULD MUCH APPRECIATE YOUR SHARING CONFIDENCE WITH HIM REGARDING NAME AND TERMS OF LONDON THEATRE CONSIDERED AND TURNED DOWN BY OLD VIC AS REPORTED IN LAST MINUTES RECEIVED stop KNOWING NOW THE REASON YOU WERE NOT ALLOWED VISIT HERE OH ME I SEE THE DOWNFALL OF OUR HOUSE LOVE = LARRY

Not until three weeks had passed did Olivier send considered replies to Esher and Burrell. By then his attitude to the Old Vic had completely changed. What a bitter pill he had to swallow. Plans for four films had been shelved in order to go on this tour: *Cyrano de Bergerac*, which would have been shot in Hollywood; a modern comedy with Vivien, to be filmed in Britain; *Othello*, again scheduled for filming in Britain; and finally—the most bizarre project of all—the life of Shakespeare. Olivier had been asked to direct this, as well as play Shakespeare—and "Hollywood-on-Avon" was to have been built in California. Vivien, instead of being more subtly cast as the Dark Lady, had been given the unlikely assignment of Anne Hathaway. She and Olivier could have earned over £3,000 a week, instead of the £60 of Old Vic salary. Yet their mood was now very dark, Michael Redington noting down—while in no way guessing at the cause—Olivier's grim observation during one understudy rehearsal, that he would be surprised "if any of them got back to England alive".

On 19 July, a Monday, the Prime Minister, Ben Chifley, came to see *The Skin of Our Teeth*. He told Elsie, whom he had met in Canberra, that she looked a great deal better than when he last saw her and that she had put on weight. Chifley himself seemed in excellent form and when he visited the Oliviers backstage he told them of a brief visit recently made to England, pronouncing it in "good shape, the countryside absolutely beautiful".

Next day Olivier spent the afternoon recording commentaries for the Red Cross, and on Wednesday he and Vivien attended a Drama League lunch where they were mobbed on arrival and on departure. Huge crowds again gathered on Friday outside the Embassy Theatre where the film *Hamlet* received its première. One schoolgirl sat above them in the balcony and thought of dropping a white kid glove at their feet. Another "sweet-talked" the caterers into letting her act as a waitress at the reception, and asked, "May I offer you a sandwich, Sir Laurence?"

The Old Vic blow had fallen on Olivier when he and Vivien had already been stretched to the limit of endurance and when, in the harsh light Sydney had turned on them, they were becoming increasingly stripped of their illusions about one another. As one correspondent explained, "Australians live in a very tough country geographically and so care less for the trimmings. Our gardens can never be what Capability Brown produced to make England the 'Sceptred Isle' it is, because out here the sun, though so cheerful a companion, is also the enemy."

Not surprisingly, signs, if only small ones, of cracks in their relationship began to appear, even to casual onlookers. In Sydney, wrote Cynthia Nolan, shadows are fiercer than substance, so that the "reflection of a chair, or wrought-iron lace, looks stronger than its original".

One such crack was revealed several days later when Olivier gave a talk about making *Hamlet* to students of Sydney University. A crowd filled the Wallace Theatre, most of it

The Bulletin

Vol. 69—No. 3569   Wednesday, July 7, 1948

IT'S BRINGING DOWN THE HOUSE

"Magnificent show, magnificent! But have you seen the Old Chif. Company doing
the 'Skin of Our Teeth'? In it I change my plumage in mid-flight."

more to see Vivien Leigh than to hear Olivier. A former veterinary student, P. L. Cunningham, recalled:

> She seemed very young, very fragile and very beautiful. She said a charming few words: commented on what an attractive picture the students made, especially the girls with their pretty faces and bright frocks—said she wished she were an artist so that she could paint the scene. She then seemed to become conscious of the fact that she was attracting too much attention away from her husband, so sat down, with the excuse that her husband was far more interesting to listen to than she was.

Insensitively—and in marked contrast to Vivien's tactful deference towards him—Olivier began to talk at length about directing Jean Simmons in Ophelia's mad scene. Simmons's casting as Ophelia had already made Vivien jealous and she now must have been again furious to be reminded of it. Olivier told his audience how he rehearsed the scene all day without being at all satisfied with the results. By this time, he reported, Simmons had grown fed up with him and would not have minded if the "sound stage roof fell in". But he had, he said, deliberately been hounding Simmons into that frame of mind, in order then to tell her how they would run through the scene once more and film it the following day. Now she had reached the stage of complete mental and physical exhaustion she gave a decent performance, "exactly as he wanted her". The take of this run-through became the sequence as finally cut. (In fact Simmons, then aged eighteen, was not very convincing whereas Vivien, though old for the part, might have been superb.)

Throughout this recitation the observant vet-to-be had his eyes closely on Vivien. "After a few minutes she seemed to realise the students were concentrating their attention on her and not really listening to her husband. She quietly moved her chair, so that she was partly in the shadows from one wing, and partly hidden from view by other people sitting on the stage. The students then concentrated on her husband." Her own thoughts, it would seem, had moved just as quietly away from Olivier.

★　　★　　★

Olivier's barber at the Australia Hotel, Mr Perc [*sic*] Ayles, described him as extremely gracious and courteous; Olivier laughed when Perc told him he would give a lock of the actor's hair to his star-struck great-niece. Perc told his friend she thought Vivien "a beautiful woman, but looked as though she had consumption". In Sydney, Vivien wore white-rimmed sunglasses most of the time and, at a Randwick race meeting, a pale pink hat, with pink gloves to match; for the Ku-ring-gai Camellia show her hat was of black straw. But little could disguise the thinness of her legs on their high heels or platform soles, and the worn, strained look on her face. Even on a private visit she made to Taronga Park Zoo newsreel cameras followed her, while one Sunday, when she and Olivier were supposed to be having a quiet day in the country, they dashed back in the late afternoon to attend a four-hour marathon at the Independent Theatre of Eugene O'Neill's *Mourning Becomes*

The Oliviers visit Taronga Park Zoo.

Electra, done by Doris Fitton's Company. Having made a detour to Centennial Park to watch part of the cricket match between the Company and the staff of the Tivoli Theatre, they were chased for speeding by a police car, and arrived at the theatre an hour late.

Because of his weakened knee Olivier had not been able to play in the match, though he said he would like to have done. His father had been a triple blue who played for the MCC although his own enthusiasm for cricket at St Edward's School, Oxford, had been dampened in the only match in which he played, by Douglas Bader bowling him out for two.

The excitement of the match was intense, even though the Company won by ten wickets. "We all feel great now that an English team has at last beaten an Australian one, on its own ground, too," wrote Redington, who captained the English side. He, as well as the Tivoli captain, wore impeccable whites; Tony Gavin bowled in suede shoes, but to good effect. Douglas Murchie, the stage manager, got a great cheer from the crowd for his green baseball cap. After dismissing the Tivoli staff for 34 the Company made 129 runs before lunch, of which Thomas Heathcote, who had played for Surrey Amateurs in 1935 and 1936, hit 97. Their innings totalled 229, but in their second innings the Tivoli side rallied, forcing the Old Vic to bat again, though they had only ten runs to make, which they did comfortably. The dramatic critic of the *Morning Herald* came along, donned umpire's coat and gave the match a neat turn of wit in next day's paper:

The match was a midwinter day's dream. Barrackers barracked in the language of Shakespeare. Instead of "Take him off", the park rang with cries of "Off with his head!" When a sixer scattered the crowd, a shrill voice cried out: "We are not safe, Clarence; we are not safe" (*Richard III*). Actor James Bailey, who took six for two in Tivoli's first innings, acted the role of Grimmett, with every delivery, "like to a bowl upon a subtle ground" (*Coriolanus*). He got his wickets so efficiently that his opponents felt they had been "bowled to death with turnips" (*Merry Wives*). But as an opening batsman, Mr Bailey failed. A rueful glance at the scorebook showed him that he was out "For O! for O!" (*Hamlet*). And his shamefaced smile cried out, "Eyes do you see? How can it be? O dainty duck! O dear!" (*Midsummer Night's Dream*).

With one out for none, actor Thomas Heathcote went to the wicket with his team-mates urging him to "dispatch those centuries to our aid" (*Coriolanus*). He lashed up 151, with 10 sixes. There were 12 ducks during the day; one of them was compiled by a batsman who was heard to say, "Like a dull actor now, I have forgot my part, and I am out even to a full disgrace" (*As You Like It*). Most of the bowlers were erratic, as if they believed "all length is torture" (*Antony*).

Early in the following week, during a performance of *Richard*, Pip Barnard had to go on as understudy and, wearing a heavy cloak, he knocked against the open keys of a piano offstage. Just when Richard was in the middle of the soliloquy, "Is there a murderer here? No . . . Yes . . ." a loud piano chord rang out between the "no" and "yes". Olivier said nothing and everyone remained terrified of repercussions until a day or two later, at a party, he went to a piano and re-enacted the whole incident. "Is there a murderer here? No . . . (launching into extravagant mock concerto, bang, bang on the piano) . . . Yes." At the weekend Olivier and Vivien escaped to a secluded house outside Sydney on the harbour at Darling Point, where they worked on the script of the broadcast of highlights from their screen and stage successes which they were going to record together in Brisbane, during the final fortnight of their stay in Australia. Their fee for this was more than £A5,000, the highest sum ever paid in Australia for a single broadcast, all of which they had decided to give to the Food for Britain Fund.

During the same "quiet" weekend Olivier wrote his formal reply to Lord Esher. Apologising for not having answered sooner, he said he had felt in need of a little time in which to think things over, and added how, in the middle of a tough job like the tour, this had been extremely difficult to find. "In spite of the delightfully charming tone of your letter, the purpose apparent in the Memorandum made me feel a little woeful and one was apt to picture oneself as a pioneer disowned by his Country in the middle of a very distant campaign." He went on that he felt thrown into confusion with regard to the future of his Australian Company, which he had been "at some pains to train to the best of my ability", for "one has become accustomed to thinking of anything for the Old Vic in terms of continuity".

He had by now realised how futile any planning for the future in a full-hearted manner had become, and he wondered what would happen about Anouilh's *Antigone*, which Burrell had forwarded some time before and whose title role Vivien had already begun to study. They had talked of opening with this at the New Theatre in February 1949, but would it now still go ahead, with the revivals of *School* and *Richard* also planned? Olivier still had ten months of his original contract to run. But what of Richardson's programme for the 1949-50 season, already quite advanced, which included Olivier as Othello, and James Bridie's *Lancelot*, in which Olivier would play Sir Lancelot and Richardson Merlin. It was all, as Olivier now wrote in a letter to John Burrell, "terribly worrying". He and Richardson, still in Hollywood, had exchanged letters and cables, showing that both were, as he told Burrell, "in the same helpless state of non-plussedness".

During his last fortnight in Sydney Olivier remained in the same mood. Vivien, for her part, cultivated serendipity, as she described it, "the gift of finding valuable or agreeable things not sought for".

The Company were ignorant of these developments: in the penultimate week each member brought three invited guests to a farewell party at Usher's hotel, and also went shopping. They marvelled at how, because of the drink laws, the police always went around in pairs. 25-year-old Anne McGrath, who played the baby mammoth in *Skin*, walking on hands and knees and waving her feet for a tail, purchased woollies and a roll-on girdle for her mother. "Sydney is a lovely place," exclaimed Redington, summing up how he and the others had had a free and easy time there.

On Thursday of the final week most of the Company

attended a ball at the Trocadero in aid of the Food for Britain appeal. Instead of packing their dresses and sending them on by sea to New Zealand, the girls had kept them out to wear, but Redington found when arriving to take his place at the top table with Olivier and Vivien that his seats were already taken, and that he had to sit with the drunks at the other end of the hall. Olivier told Redington that he "had never been so terrified anywhere . . . everyone was drunk except the governor and the people just stood on the tables and stared at them". Redington further and indignantly noted that they did not play dance tunes but "army march tunes at brisk dance tempo". But the last drink they had with the Tivoli staff, when they gave them a cricket bat signed by all the Company, proved a much more pleasant occasion.

Eight years earlier when Olivier left the stage for the Fleet Air Arm, he thought he was abandoning his frivolous and empty-headed fellow artists for a more genuine class of person. But he soon discovered the extent of his mistake. The revelation grew in him not only that "acting can be a very good training for living", but that "the most real, the most affectionate, the most sincere people in the world are actors".

Since that time Olivier had always sought the company of other theatre people and, owing to the persistence of a Sydney producer, John Kay, he and Vivien did finally see in action —though for only four days before they left for Brisbane—an outstanding local actor. It was an irony that, while Olivier had been doing his best to encourage theatre in Australia and while other notables like Doris Fitton had been stressing the urgency, during the Oliviers' visit, of Australia building her own theatres, Olivier's own first reaction on seeing this actor, Peter Finch, on 18 August was at once to encourage him to leave for England. He went even further, and offered him a three-year contract with Laurence Olivier Productions, the £100 limited liability company he had formed in 1947 with his agent, Cecil Tennant, as its manager. How could he be so inconsistent? But to be fair, Finch himself thought by this time that he had exhausted all the possibilities for the expansion of his career that existed in Australia.

When the Oliviers saw Finch he was playing Argan in a

fifty-minute version of Molière's *The Imaginary Invalid,*★ for the Mercury Mobile Players. The performance took place at lunchtime in the joinery shop of Frank G. O'Brien's Glass Works in Waterloo, a Sydney suburb, where they sat in an audience of 450 factory workers who responded informally while munching sandwiches and drinking coffee. Commented Olivier:

> It was a magnificent idea. It really was theatre for the people, to think of taking it to their place of work. That's going right back to the beginnings of theatre. Instead of having people come to a particular theatre, what an audience you can reach, and without their having to sit through long plays.

How could Olivier want to be seen as encouraging Australia, on the one hand, to build up its own companies, and at the same time remove by the force of his own allure and prestige the one actor capable of being a spearhead in that development? Olivier said, according to Finch's biographer Trader Faulkner, "I knew from the moment I saw him in Sydney that he could become one of the truly gifted actors of our time," and certainly Finch was a fine example of the natural actor. Surely, then, all the more reason to leave him in Australia? But Olivier was now increasingly thinking of himself as a manager: "Practicability is my god," he once told the actress Fabia Drake, "and adaptability the most natural of the human ways of this."

Finch immediately took up Olivier's offer, but if he had been capable of seeing ahead further he might never have uttered the statement, "Mercury was the dead-end of an evolutionary process", and left a whole virgin area of development offered by Australian theatre in order to trail to Britain after the Oliviers. Yet, far from being a "discovery" of Olivier's, he had been a professional actor for fourteen years, and had made some seven or eight films, while all through the war he had acted and produced for the troops, ending as Artistic Director of Unit 12, the Australian Army's equivalent

---

★ In his autobiography Olivier mistakenly recalled his first meeting with Finch as taking place in Melbourne, and the play as *Tartuffe*.

of ENSA. By the time of the Old Vic tour he had been for some years a household name in Australia. "I've buggered up my own career," he later told Faulkner, "by going off all over the world, but I feel the urge to live my way as greatly as I feel the need to act."

Nonetheless in his autobiography Olivier claimed that "in the normal process of talent-scouting we had heard high praise of this young man's work". But were there subconscious reasons why a famous man of forty-one, clearly tired and feeling his personal life with his wife was not all it could be, should pick a staggeringly handsome man of thirty-two to join his immediate circle? Olivier had now grown aware of looking older than his years. According to the actor Harcourt Williams, quoted in Audrey Williamson's *Theatre of Two Decades*, he was undergoing mid-life crisis:

> Larry had lost the basic need that propels every actor. He was leaning more and more towards directing and producing, because he no longer had the drive for attention . . . his attitude to life was almost world-weary . . . That's the most singular aspect of his character that I recall at that time: sobriety, and a tinge of sadness, resignation.

In Finch he saw himself ten years younger; he liked Finch's brashness, his apparent innocence. What made Finch seem to him even younger than his actual years, was the fact that, in contrast to himself, Finch was unknown in the wider world. Olivier wanted, again, to possess that vitality of being on the outside trying to break in. As well as an engaging streak of vulgarity, Finch had a disarming insolence that made him in no way prepared to kowtow to fame and stardom; he possessed, in abundance, those qualities Olivier praised in actors: sincerity, affection, "reality".

Vivien saw in Finch a striking young courtier, a potential favourite, perhaps more dangerous by virtue of his talent and looks than Dan Cunningham or any other. She sensed that he shared with her an attachment to those same elements of passion that had, in the first instance, drawn herself and Olivier together. Like recognises like. No one could be better qualified to join the entourage, and in their last few days in

Sydney Finch quickly became part of the Oliviers' social scene. He also joined them in a hastily prepared interstate network broadcast which they gave just prior to leaving Sydney.

There may have been looks exchanged, or other portents of what followed between 1949 and 1954. Finch, like Olivier and Vivien before they met, was married; and later Olivier claimed that he had "encouraged it [Vivien's attraction towards Finch] oh, quite innocently at first". But if Vivien's later affair with Finch became a dramatically exaggerated symptom of the failure of the relationship with Olivier, there were already in August 1948 more clear signs of Vivien's dissatisfaction with the state of her marriage. Towards the end of the Sydney run she grew both physically and emotionally frayed, and her fatigue bordered on neurasthenia: she undoubtedly needed to "break out", but had no alternative other than to allow her body and nerves to absorb the stress. Olivier's depression over his treatment by the Old Vic governors further served to isolate her.

She went on at the Tivoli for the final performances ill and trembling with overstrain. After the last matinee of *The School for Scandal* on Saturday, Elsie Beyer, temporarily reassuming her role as governess, escorted a grim-looking Vivien from the stage door into her car. Untypically, Vivien did not smile at the large crowd gathered outside. Between the shows she went straight to bed and even after the evening performance, when the corridor outside her dressing room was choked with flowers, she and Olivier shunned the crowds gathered to bid them farewell.

"Miss Leigh is quite exhausted," commented Olivier curtly.

2   Brisbane

Brisbane came as a relief after Sydney, not least because they had sent on the heavy scenery to New Zealand, and performed, as in Perth, only *The School for Scandal*. The final fortnight in Australia passed much the same as the one with which they had begun.

While the Oliviers spent Sunday morning resting and flew in the afternoon to Brisbane, most of the remainder of the Company, to their annoyance, boarded a train: "God save me from the Australian train, they are the worst things ever," remarked Redington. But on arrival everyone settled comfortably into a temperance hotel, finding it clean and with excellent service.

The Oliviers stayed at Lennon's Hotel. After their short rest they seemed replenished with their usual smiles, no doubt relieved they had to perform only the one play. But Brisbane was less than happy with this arrangement: jealousy between states being common in Australia, the Queenslanders felt snubbed. "We are Shakespeare-starved here," complained the Repertory Society Vice-President, while the Brisbane Shakespearean Society President would have liked to have seen *Richard III*—even performed on a bare stage without scenery. To make things worse, the posters advertising the Company in Brisbane had listed all three plays.

Dan O'Connor had to make a public statement. *School*, he explained, showed the whole Company to best effect, and even to bring this to Brisbane had cost £A10,000 above normal running costs. (£A3,000 alone had been spent on air-freighting scenery.) But for its commitment to Brisbane, O'Connor pointed out, the Company could have had a much longer season in Sydney. Backstage, just for eleven performances of *School*, Bill Bundy supervised the unloading and installation of electrical fittings valued at £A40,000 and which filled twenty large packing cases. Everybody, in particular the stage staff under Kentish, and the wardrobe staff under Emma Selby-Walker, worked well into the night.

In the end, as Perth had at the beginning of the tour, Brisbane bowed gracefully before *The School for Scandal*, turning out for the first night in the now expected and mixed

"Is Old Vic. in?"

A Brisbane viewpoint.

display of finery. But the unkinder critics played sharply and with truth upon Olivier's evident fatigue. "Not once, during the entire performance," wrote Warwick Lawrence in the *Telegraph*, "did the virile dynamic assert himself. He was the creaking, rheumatic, fussing good-hearted old benedick." But for Lawrence the critic Vivien still shone brightly—or at least buzzed: "always the hornet . . . in and out of her husband's periwig". Doris Waraker expressed her reservation bluntly—"We could be content with an even younger Sir Peter than Olivier has given us in this beautiful performance" —while "Penny Plain" waxed literary: "the fine cadences of Olivier's voice, reminiscent of Sir Thomas Browne's prose in *Urn Burial*, harmonise with the rich colourings of the men's costumes in wine-red, peach and cornflower blue".

Socially, too, after the stress of Sydney, Brisbane provided the Company with a welcome anti-climax. News of their cricket match against the Tivoli staff had travelled ahead of them, and their team, still with Redington as captain, was challenged by the Brisbane Wanderers. This time the opposition lined up some top-class cricketers: everyone in the Wanderers had played for Queensland, and though most were "rather elderly", wrote Redington, one of them, G. G. Cook, had scored 169 not out against the MCC only two years before. The Brisbane Test ground was made available and here, to the Old Vic team's awe and amazement, the groundsman fussed over the pitch, complaining that it was not good enough. The Wanderers won the toss, went in to bat and scored 171 for five wickets before declaring. Taking three wickets, and out of a total of 61 making 37 runs, Thomas Heathcote again proved the mainstay of the Old Vic team. During their second innings time ran out so the actual result was a face-saving draw.

They had arrived in Perth in a late summer heatwave; now in Brisbane, centre of Australia's most fertile belt, they were in a tropical rain season. Again the weather grew warm: spring was in the air, daffodils opening, and Elsie perked up, changing the tint of her glasses from dark brown to the lightest of blues. She sported yet another Jacqmar headscarf inscribed in Afrikaans and English, this one designed to commemorate the Royal Tour of South Africa: "one of the luxuries I do allow myself". She and the rest much enjoyed a trip up the Brisbane River to Moreton Bay laid on by the Royal Queensland Yacht Club. Leaving in nine launches, they ate a picnic lunch on Bishop Island, and from the island swam in warm water, enjoying the hot sun which emerged after rain.

The day after, sixteen of the Company had an even better excursion; at five o'clock in the morning they were driven to the Great Dividing Range, where they arrived at nine to be treated at a "bush" breakfast to the best steaks they had ever eaten. The panorama of rich black earth stretching in all directions amazed them and they reflected that here, at last, they could see the real Australia that they had read about, with farming properties extending for miles and straight roads vanishing to a pin point. After calling in at Warwick, the very slow and dusty, but charming country town which was the centre of this area, they returned via Cunningham's Gap, through which they beheld a wonderful vista in which the afternoon sun shone down brilliantly on the whole Dividing Range. To make their day even more remarkable, a baby wild kangaroo, the first they had seen, crossed their path.

That same night, after the performance, the Oliviers, again "royals" by proxy, attended the St George's Society Ball at Cloudland Ballroom where, while they stood, he in white tie and tails, she in long silk gown and mink stole, twenty-nine debutantes filed past and shook hands with them. Vivien performed the ceremony of cutting the debutantes' cake, then they both sat down behind a screen to a much needed four-course dinner. By now they had reached the small hours of 31 August, the day of their eighth wedding anniversary.

After sleep they spent the remainder of their anniversary quietly: in each it may have given rise to some silent and woeful reflection. He still wore the topaz ring she had given him, inscribed "La fidelité ma guide": his message, on her wedding ring, had been blunter: "This is the last one you'll get, I hope."

The sense of anti-climax and relaxation continued through the second week, too. Yet another rally organised in aid of Food for Britain had a poor response, producing only three truckloads of tinned food. The children who turned up said they hadn't come to see the Oliviers but the speedway cars, which were "beaut". They also visited a TB Hospital. After an address given by Olivier to students of the University of Queensland in George Street, a professor stood up and asked why the Company had not brought all three plays to Brisbane. "I can still remember the look of restrained impatience and annoyance which passed over the face of Sir Laurence Olivier as he turned to reply," recalled the Students' Union Vice-President.

The wistful calm of these final days was soon broken, but from another quarter. Every week since Vivien had left England she had received a letter "from" her Siamese cat, New, giving a complete weekly bulletin of his life and doings which either her secretary or personal maid had written. New had signed them with a smudge from his paw. But the week before the Oliviers left Brisbane New was driven by car from Durham Cottage for a holiday in Notley. A few days later he ran out of the front gate where he was knocked over by a car and killed.

Receiving this information in Brisbane by cable distressed Vivien greatly. Olivier had given her New four years before on her birthday, since when New had gone everywhere with her, even to the theatre where he watched her dress and make up. She had wanted to bring him to Australia, but quarantine regulations had forbidden it. When passing through Archerfield for the first time she had befriended—on the airfield tarmac—a small substitute cat. Seeing the same cat again this time made it seem like a ghost sent to pursue them. Quickly, without letting her know, Olivier cabled his London secretary, Dorothy Welford, with instructions to buy for their return a little Siamese kitten to replace New.

The Oliviers gave the final broadcast which they had been preparing since July on 4 September. After a considerable amount of behind-the-scenes string-pulling which had ended in a direct appeal from Olivier to the Prime Minister, the Company had been granted permission to fly scenery and equipment direct from Brisbane to Auckland in a chartered Skymaster. At first the Civil Aviation Director-General refused to allocate sufficient petrol, but he later relented. Olivier and Vivien, rather than return to Sydney to join the regular flight on which the rest of the Company had been booked, opted to fly on the Skymaster. "I must say there seems to be a tremendous amount of stuff to pack into that aircraft," wrote Elsie Beyer, "and I only hope it remains airborne."

The captain of this unscheduled flight was Keith Virtue, a pilot of 20,000 hours' flying experience; the hostess, Anne Chandler, welcomed her distinguished passengers on board, settling them into their seats for the eleven-hour flight across the Tasman Sea. Olivier's height appeared less than she had imagined it. She noted how pale Vivien looked on boarding the plane, and attributed it to too much party-going and to her dislike of flying. But Anne found herself in no way prepared for what happened halfway through the journey when they were flying over the water at 11,000 feet. Suddenly Vivien became breathless and started fighting for air. The pilot quickly brought the plane down to 4,000 feet, and fortunately on board they had a portable oxygen mask which Anne applied to Vivien's face.

The emergency gave everyone on the plane a nasty shock. Although Vivien perked up considerably by the end of the flight, diving in and out of her colossal Elizabeth Arden make-up case, and spending hours on her face (leaving used cotton-wool balls behind the window curtain, which gave the aircraft a delightful aroma, said Anne), her sudden attack again threw attention on to her underlying frailty.

"Why is it that in troubled times one's body feels called upon to jump on to the bandwagon?" asked Olivier once again.

PART FOUR

The Eye of Heaven

I want to deceive him just enough to make him want me.

Blanche in *A Streetcar Named Desire*

1   New Zealand

In Sydney, Olivier had tried to get Vivien to go and have an x-ray and check-up: she replied that she would—later. She insisted she was not ill; and this remained an article of faith. If disease and despair were a form of depravity, or a judgment of God, Vivien, still in reaction against her Catholic upbringing, seemed with an almost atheistic defiance not to heed the warnings.

Upon arrival in Auckland, however, she did accept the necessity for treatment, which she received at Green Lane Hospital. "Poor little thing, how tired her sickness must have made her. At times she looked so ethereal, just as though she was going to float away," commented Doreen McKay, a student at Dunedin University. Vivien needed all the strength that she could muster, for now, crammed into the final five weeks of the tour, in the four main centres of Auckland, Christchurch, Dunedin, and Wellington, they had to give nearly fifty performances, multiplying and concentrating the problems of packing and unpacking clothes, sets, and equipment—testing, as never before, the mobility and stage-worthiness of the full repertoire, even to the extent of staging, within an eight-day period in two different places, all three plays.

In this Herculean labour they had one immense psychological advantage: they knew, at the end of it, they would be going home, and—for the twenty-eight lucky ones who were chosen—they knew they had another month at sea on the *Corinthic*. After weeks of rumour, with negotiations and alternative plans rising and falling, the arrangements for the return passage were, during the first few days in Auckland, at last confirmed. The *Corinthic* seemed now, to that stage-weary group, after all their protracted toil, the promised land. Yet even on the *Corinthic* there would be more work to do. By cable and letter Olivier had settled with Burrell and with the Old Vic governors who, in conciliatory mood after letters exchanged in July and early August, had agreed that in the January-to-June season in 1949 the Company would still play at the New Theatre. They would, as planned, open with *School*, then revive *Richard*, and, as the third play, substituting for *Skin*, Anouilh's *Antigone* would get its first London production.

Aboard the *Corinthic*, *School* and *Richard* could take a well-earned rest, but *Antigone* had to be started from scratch. Olivier went ahead with the preparations. He cast George Relph as Creon, himself as the Chorus, and Dan Cunningham as Antigone's fiancé Haemon.

A particular challenge for Vivien, the part of Antigone offered a modern, and possibly ideal—because lightweight —tragic role. Anouilh's heroine did not rampage in the traditional manner: her defiance was understated and cerebral yet cunningly theatrical—designed by Anouilh as a symbol of the French resistance to the German occupation. Vivien, with her instinctive liking for France, and her knowledge of the language and literature, could prove outstanding. But the natural timbre of her voice remained high-pitched and slight; so, too, did her stage timing have a quickness which underlined wit more than feeling. She still needed to develop technically for the stage the depth which, with no apparent effort, she could project on the screen. No one knew better how to help her achieve this than Olivier.

He was pleased with the improvements in technique she had made during the tour. He thought in particular that she had developed the naturalistic side of Lady Teazle and built, in the two quarrel scenes, the means of achieving effective climaxes. When he contemplated further his dismissal by the Old Vic he realised how an increase in Vivien's range, especially in tragedy, in which he would have liked her to be his equal, made any new company they might now form a stronger proposition. His hopes again rose of a stage partnership as successful as that of Alfred Lunt and Lynn Fontanne. Viewed in terms of his relationship with the Old Vic, his dismissal made the present tour seem an expensive labour in pursuit of the lost ideal of a National Theatre; considered as the pilot enterprise of a newborn actor-manager's company, its trials and problems once again could become a challenge of leadership.

Not that he had ever wavered in his loyalty to the tour and the Company. He had forged this Company into a unified whole, and *School* had, up to then, been his own most accomplished stage production. On their return to London the public and press would have the chance to see what the governors had jettisoned in favour of the social ideals of equality and company spirit.

Cecil Tennant had, moreover, forwarded to Australia a new play for Vivien; they had now both read it and were sure it had in it the perfect part for her. It was by the author of *The Glass Menagerie*, Tennessee Williams. They had wired Cecil to tell Hugh Beaumont, who had an option on the play, that they were interested and decided provisionally, after the termination of their contracts at the New, to make it one of the first productions of their new venture into management. Its title was *A Streetcar named Desire*.

In 1948 not only was New Zealand geographically the most isolated country in the world, it had also virtually no living culture of its own. On Saturday nights most people went along to the pictures, so the Oliviers were, as in Australia, household names. But many people had never been to a "straight" play, much less one by Shakespeare, while *The School for Scandal* was an unknown quantity. The rare commercial theatres that visited New Zealand from Australia played very safe, although in Auckland in particular an enterprising amateur theatrical movement had stirred. As in Australia, alongside a nostalgia for Great Britain, a strong residual desire for theatre existed. New Zealand, too, as a loyal colony, felt starved of royal visits—no "royals" had toured since the Duke and Duchess of Gloucester in the mid 1930s —and therefore the "substitute royal" factor of the Oliviers was again to play an enormous part in their attraction.

But now, like overhunted game, wounded and harassed, the "royal" pair had grown wary of breaking cover. If on arrival at Whenuapai airport they could not avoid signing a few autographs they made up for it later by pleading tiredness and their heavy theatrical duties, and so escaping the crippling round of social engagements they had suffered in Australia. Almost at once a local admirer of Vivien's, Sir Ernest Davis, began sending round daily to the Grand Hotel, where she and Olivier stayed while in Auckland, a huge bouquet of flowers. But Davis respected their privacy and placed at their disposal a chauffeur-driven car. In 1961, when Vivien visited New Zealand again, though this time without Olivier, Davis took her sailing on his luxury yacht: when he eventually died he left her in his will a considerable sum.

The others had flown out of Brisbane on the scheduled airline flight to Auckland via Sydney. In Sydney some of them had transferred to a seaplane: on boarding it they were met by their pilot, holding a cigarette in his shaking hand: "Isn't this fun?" he told them. "We've never taken off at night!" Delayed by engine trouble, they did not leave harbour until 2 am. At first sight they found New Zealand to be just like home: "very very much like England", wrote Redington, "so green and so many trees we have not seen for so long . . . no gum trees, no palms, but lots of hedges". People who served in shops were polite (and spoke without Australian accents). In contrast to Sydney, they saw little drunkenness or wild behaviour.

Two of the single men in the Company, James Bailey and John ("Pip") Barnard, had decided to return and stay in Australia after the end of the tour and try and find work there—mainly, they hoped, in radio. They had asked Olivier for their release and he had granted this.

Though their initial enthusiasm for New Zealand was strong, after a short time the Company missed the colour of Sydney and its free and easy style. Most again found billets with private families, and these, combined with long hours at the theatre and little free time, grew onerous, especially when their hosts wanted to talk. Redington complained, in their first week, that they had three matinées and three rehearsals. After six months he and most of the remainder had grown tired of sightseeing, and he also soon felt weary of his Auckland host's three daughters, none of whom especially caught his eye. "As terrifying as ever," he commented, especially the sex-starved one whom "poor John [Barnard] had to look after . . . as he is good at that sort of thing." But a 25 per cent rise in the New Zealand pound which boosted their salaries to the level they were paid in Australia (and to parity with sterling), compensated, and so did the prospect of returning to England: "Sir

Laurence called us together the other day and quoted a very famous line, 'within a month'."

Hard work again ruled. More than 33,000 people attended the seventeen performances they gave at St James's Theatre, Auckland, where seats ranged in price from five shillings to a guinea. With takings at more than £20,000 they established the world record for a repertory season—£2,000 more, claimed Ian Donald, the theatre manager, than the 1938 record in Chicago of Katherine Cornell in *The Barretts of Wimpole Street*. Donald pointed to two exceptional factors: the revaluation of the New Zealand pound and the great size of the theatre, which seated 2,000 (unlike the Capitol, Perth, it had a back wall, so to the actors it felt only half the size). Clive Woods, when handed the "returns" for the first night, thought it must all be "paper" (complimentary tickets), but it was not. What particularly heartened everyone, however, was not only the size of the audience but its quality. Utterly rapt and attentive, it made individual performances improve, especially in *Richard III* and in particular Olivier's.

Final-year pupils of the "co-ed" Takapuna Grammar School on North Shore were asked by their teachers to write essays on the productions so that the best could be chosen for the school magazine. In her submission, "K. T." of VIa wrote of *School*: "Although the characterisation in the play is not very deep, the characters tending to be types rather than individuals, each actor so lives his part that the characters live, think, and feel as real people and become something more than make-believe." Lady Olivier, continued K. T., gave a brilliant performance "by merely intensifying her own provocative kittenish personality". That Olivier had recovered, as Richard, the energy and zest he had lost in Sydney impressed nineteen-year-old Brian Fisher: in particular the look on his face as he died "leaning sideways on his arm, the anguish and passion of that look is something never to be forgotten".

Saying he and "Viv" in Australia had tried to do too much, Olivier graciously excused himself from the social round: "I became ill and had to miss some performances and so did Viv." But they made an exception and visited Auckland University College: here Vivien wore a dress of Gordon tartan, a long-sleeved bodice—with an emerald and diamond fob pinned to it—a skirt of unpressed pleats, and a wide-brimmed, crownless black hat. When she walked with Olivier to the hall from the main entrance, deep lines of students pressed in on her. But to Iris Winchester, who was present on that occasion, the fine black veil tied over her face marred her appearance, causing Iris shock and disappointment— in New Zealand veils were not fashionable. "It not only hid her from those whose only wish was to admire, but gave an alarming first impression of disfigurement." At one cinema, where a film of hers was running, Vivien was advertised on the poster outside as "Sir Laurence Olivier's Crown Jewel of the Old Vic Company".

At University College the Oliviers took part in the opening ceremony for a new staff common room. "Most potent, grave, and reverend signiors, my very noble and approved good masters," quoted Vivien, adding, "I think that is about as much of the role of Othello as I shall ever be called upon to say." She then declared that it seemed an uncommonly lovely room and that she had "enormous pleasure in declaring it absolutely open".

Because of exceptionally bad weather the journey from Auckland to Christchurch was delayed: Olivier and Vivien left on the last of three planes, but the sky had cleared when they came down to refuel at Wellington, where tea was served to passengers. At Christchurch airport a very large crowd had assembled which the Oliviers managed to dodge, but Larry himself did not escape the single press man who called on him in the evening at the United Services Hotel, where he and Vivien had first been given a room with two single beds. They insisted on a double-bed which "they were old-fashioned enough to prefer".

The winter of 1948 in Christchurch had been severe, and as an after-effect of the war people were still very run-down. Hotel dining-rooms shut at nine o'clock, so the Oliviers had to engage someone to serve them supper in their room. On Monday morning they paid a courtesy call on the Mayor and Mayoress of Christchurch, but in the unheated St James's Theatre in the afternoon, as they prepared to open *School* the same evening, tempers became very frayed. Unpacking the costumes took a long time, and in front of three temporary theatre staff, Pam Mann, Bridget Lenihan, and Barbara Pack-wood, who were helping in the basement by placing clothes in piles and on hangers, the Oliviers had a blazing row during which they made little attempt to restrain their language.

The cause was Lady Teazle's red shoes, which could not be found anywhere: instead of gracefully accepting a substitute Vivien stormed at the staff who cowered before her brilliant green eyes, flashing at them from below stage eyelashes. Before the girls could escape Olivier himself appeared, telling Vivien she was late and to grab any shoes and get up on stage.

Only moments later, after her refusal, and calling her a bitch, he slapped her face and at once she hit him back, referring to him as a "bastard" for hitting her—and submit-ting the girls to the embarrassment of watching a full-scale battle of wills. This was the first time the underlying hostility each felt emerged publicly in front of stage staff. Olivier finally reduced her to submission by reminding her of her desertion of her first husband and child. "We never did find the red shoes," said Barbara Packwood, "they must have been left in Wellington."

In spite of the row, and in spite of the bad feeling between them that still existed as a result—and which only increased Vivien's growing sense of isolation—the opening of *School*, though punctuated by the coughs and sniffles of a shivering audience, went most successfully. Though mutual confidence had been badly shaken, it would seem, and Vivien stirred up with guilt and wounded vanity, they never openly quarrelled again on the tour. It must have required an effort not to air their grievances before the "family", but Company spirit remained an inviolable bond, bringing out the best in them, while clearly they were determined to keep up the outward show of love and affection towards each other. That night the scenes between Sir Peter and Lady Teazle dazzled with their polish and professionalism:

Sir Peter: No, no, madam: 'tis evident you never cared a pin for me, and I was a madman to marry you—a pert, rural coquette, that had refused half the honest 'squires in the neighbourhood!
Lady Teazle: And I am sure I was a fool to marry you . . .

But Olivier and Vivien were now probably aware of the cruelty lying just beneath the surface, while the tension both pushed down had to emerge somewhere.

And so it did only two days later when Olivier played Richard. Again the stabbing pain in the apparently straight knee; again that feeling of being held in a vice. Cursing, he once more got out the crutch, and cut the fight at the end. Again he had an injection of morphine to help him through the evening performance. But now he knew and accepted that something had to be done to settle the problem. He enquired about having an operation either in Wellington, the last town on the tour, or in London immediately on their return. Time was short: only three weeks after their arrival back in England they had to open again at the New Theatre.

The resurgence of Olivier's old pain did little to help soothe Vivien's feelings of resentment towards him, which grew rather than diminished, so that later he would say, "Somehow, somewhere on this tour I knew that Vivien was lost to me."

On Monday 27 September after the show, both attended a performance by the Canterbury University Club Dramatic Society of one act of Pirandello's *Six Characters in Search of an Author*, produced by Ngaio Marsh, the thriller writer. Olivier propped his leg on a footstool and from the effects of pain and pain-killers appeared to doze. But the Old Vic personnel thought the production highly proficient: several names were jotted down for possible Old Vic studentships.

Vivien's own tension from the week found relief in a highly sexy, and, for the times, daring outfit: a revealing black dress split to the waist. A gesture of defiance towards Olivier, it caused the stir which she intended—as well as putting her health at risk yet again. How did those lines from that new play of Tennessee Williams run? "People don't see you—men don't—don't even admit your existence unless they are making love to you."

But the "family", did not suffer. In spite of the poor weather, in spite of Larry's resurgent affliction, those with birthdays in August and September still had their celebration: this time the picnic lunch had to be diverted back to the Oliviers' flat in their hotel. "There was Sir Laurence lying in

bed, in marvellous silk pyjamas, cutting two huge hams,"
wrote Michael Redington. After masses to eat and drink they
disappeared (minus Olivier) in two coaches into the countryside: the rain dried up, and the sun shone on the fields of newly
opened daffodils, making beautiful shadows over the hills.

What a strange year of seasonal confusion Olivier and
Vivien were passing through: a cold dreary winter had given
way to tropical late summer, then a mild wet winter, then
tropical mid-winter summer heat in Sydney and Brisbane, and
now a cold, temperate spring: awaiting them, on their return
to London, was their third winter of the year. Three winters
and not a single summer.

Their love could not but now be at risk. They had no
separations planned which might in the former way reinforce
it. Olivier had more and more the feeling that, as he wrote
later, he was being "condemned to death". Painfully he began
to learn

> . . . Apostasie of her
> Who taught me first idolatry.

2   The Operation

Floy Bell, their secretary, and the Relphs, Mercia and George,
accompanied them from Christchurch on the car drive to
Dunedin, a town in the South Island where many of the local
people were of Scots extraction and educational standards
were high. Arriving at five o'clock they drove straight to the
City Hotel where Vivien, dressed in black, looking pale and
delicate, made a balcony appearance, waving to the crowd

gathered below. A short time later, the car drove her and Olivier straight from the hotel into the scene dock of His Majesty's Theatre, where *School*, performed as in Hobart with only tabs and stage-cloths, opened.

The sophistication and excellence of the performance again overwhelmed the local people, who also enjoyed the impeccable team work. "One scene red and velvet, curtain rosy glow; black silhouettes behind drop," wrote Doreen McKay in impressionistic style. "Tall, black wrought-iron candelabrum used, never seen the likes before or since, to throw light flambeau style." Of another scene: "Men at table drinking . . . dressed in soft dove grey velvet . . . colouring beautiful, lighting red . . . like the expression on Olivier's face (so natural) when he looked behind the screen to find his wife."

After the performance twelve of the Company attended a mayoral reception, which, reported Elsie tartly, "seemed to be a big success". Next day Olivier, as widely reported, said as Vivien stood next to him, her arm through his, "You may not know it, but you are talking to two walking corpses."

In Dunedin it never stopped raining so that by the end of the week, having been on Friday also buffeted by gales and hailstones, most of them were only too glad to leave. One local woman told Olivier she had been every night to see *Hamlet*, also showing that week in Dunedin: he laughed and said, "Surely you are not right in the head!" At another time he found himself confronted by his double: a distant cousin called Olivier who was the spitting image of him, but he seemed unconcerned at the portent. Dunedin's hospitality, however, made up for the inclement weather: on leaving, some of the Company found their money refused by their hosts; also they began to stock-pile food, such as Christmas cakes of rich ingredients, to take back to England.

In Wellington, the state capital, where the rest of the scenery had travelled direct from Christchurch, they were caught by the fierce wind blowing up Cook Strait from the Antarctic, but at least they now had the *Corinthic* in view: on first sighting her at anchor while they were travelling in a coach and had just taken a bend—all had cheered. "I'm staying," wrote Redington, "in a house in Oriental Bay: from the house is a lovely view of the whole harbour, and there, right across the harbour on the other side of the Bay, is the *Corinthic*. So if I see it creeping out one morning I shall swim after it, no matter how cold the water is, or what state I am in! I've waited for eight months for the boat home and I am not going to miss it now!" But, he added in plaintive tone, sailing had been postponed by two days. "I pray it will not be postponed any more." A journalist from a Wellington paper also noticed how everyone looked frantically for mail from home as they passed the letter rack at the theatre.

Redington found Wellington rather like Hull, but so pre-occupied did he grow with the idea of returning home that he had no time to decide whether or not he liked it: casting uneasy glances at the wharf-workers he worried over their system of remuneration. They got paid, he complained, even when it rained and as a result they did no work: what in heaven would he and the Company do if they went on strike? But in terms of the diplomatic fuss it would cause, a strike was unlikely, especially as Olivier, hobbling now between plays in growing pain and anguish, had to officiate like a "royal" at a few final functions, including a "Morning Tea", served at 11.45 am, where he addressed the New Zealand parliament.

Causing at least one hungry and high-ranking churchman surreptitiously to help himself to a slice of mouth-watering cream sponge, the Oliviers arrived a little late. "Do not think of us," said Olivier in a witty, at times caustic speech, which reminded one listener of Lord Louis Mountbatten, "as two leading players and a cast of supporting actors, but as a complete company working with the idea of unity." In spite of this the Acting Prime Minister, Walter Nash, replied in terms specifically flattering to the pair, with the observation that when people looked at Vivien they were inclined even to forget her famous husband. Olivier agreed:

> I have become so accustomed to seeing faces falling about three yards when I appear anywhere alone that I am forever reminded of my wife's appeal. But I know how they feel—when I think of Vivien Leigh I find it impossible to think of anything else.

These apparently heartfelt words were echoed by a spokesman

for the ethnic minority, T. T. Ropiha: the Maori people, he said, appreciated the Oliviers' visit even more than the Pakehas (white New Zealanders). This remark brought forth a murmur of denial. "We are trying to preserve the best in Maori culture without the influence of the Pakeha, and yours is the same idea in preserving British culture. Your high regard for the maintenance of your own culture is akin to our own."

"My prefects! I'm horrified!" the headmistress of a girls' school declared in alarm on seeing a group of her top girls clustering round the windows of Parliament House, waving at Olivier. The Prime Minister soothed her: "I think that's very enterprising of them."

Very enterprisingly, too, the Oliviers managed to make an appetising fish follow them from Dunedin to Wellington. Having noticed that the fishing season had opened in Dunedin, Olivier had asked the hotel proprietress to provide trout for dinner. None could be found but Otago went on trying until, only just before their departure, an inspector of fisheries caught a five-pounder. In the rush of leaving it was left behind, but it was sent on to Wellington where, on their second night, they devoured it with relish.

For Olivier—who, wrote Nancy Steer, had arrived at the St George's Hotel looking "rather grim", in contrast to Vivien, "so beautiful in a pretty hat, smiling sweetly at us in the hall"—it supplied spit enough at least for *Richard III*, the last performances of which on the tour occurred in the middle of the first week. On seeing Olivier as Richard, Mrs Steer wrote of an erotic bonus: in the delivery of those first wonderful lines "a little spot of spittle sprang from his lip and landed on my lap".

On Saturday 9 October fell the last performance of *The Skin of Our Teeth*: in a curtain speech Olivier, with emotion, told how it had been his and Vivien's first joint success. They bequeathed the costumes and sets to the local repertory company. This final night increased the sense of melancholy, especially as Olivier, since his knee had now "locked", had arranged for his operation to take place after the following Monday's performance of *School*. During his stay in hospital three more performances of *School* were to be added to the programme, with Derrick Penley as Teazle (the official understudy, Hugh Stewart, had fallen ill). Olivier rehearsed Penley, a grandson of W. S. Penley who wrote *Charley's Aunt*, who had only five days' notice to play the part, with extreme care:

> We learnt [wrote Redington] more about the production in that one rehearsal than we had done in the whole tour. Sir Laurence is wonderful, and of course you can see how good he is when someone else is playing his part, though Derrick is very good indeed. The thing one notices so much about Larry is how delicate he is and how he does not waste one gesture or inflection.

As well as chronicling the end-of-tour shadows with nostalgic tenderness, Redington also kept his steadfast eye on the *Corinthic*, happy that towards the end of their stay the weather was improving, making the chance of a wharf strike less likely.

After the Monday performance the Company gathered in maudlin fashion to say goodbye to Larry, even though the parting was to last only four nights. They gave Larry and Viv a present; George Relph made a very moving speech, which so affected Larry that, hardly able to utter a few choked words, he went and kissed George. Everyone else wept too, Vivien among them. It was all "rather silly", wrote Redington, especially as they still had the journey home and another six months of acting together, but they had become totally devoted to Olivier. Pip Barnard and Redington sent him a note, wishing him a "very successful opening in the other theatre". Next morning at the Lewisham Private Hospital in Florence Street he was put to sleep by Sister Slater of the Little Company of Mary. After a neat excision the ruptured cartilage of his right knee was removed: just in time to avoid the likelihood of permanent disablement, said the distinguished surgeon, Kennedy Elliott, making it a condition that Olivier should not put his weight on this leg for the first two weeks of the voyage home.

In hospital many of the Company visited him: he made crude jokes with the young men about the delicacies involved in being confined to bed and having to call on nuns for assistance.

On the very last night of *School* Vivien, in a farewell speech from the stage, declaimed, "Farewell, Wellington! Farewell New Zealand! Farewell Australasia!" and then in her marvellous Cecil Beaton gown did the lowest curtsey ever. When told of this Olivier, like a doting father, looked proud of Vivien's achievement and almost wept again. On Friday night, as the crew made final preparations for sailing the next morning, 16 October, at 8 am, the Company minus Olivier boarded the *Corinthic*. With them they brought all the food they could possibly carry on board. That same evening the hospital staff strapped Olivier's leg in plaster and from the balcony of Room 49 he and Vivien made a farewell broadcast: "It became a classic," said a local resident, "as the background sounded as if the banshees were out—our well-known Wellington wind!"

Next morning, half an hour before sailing time, the hospital porters placed Olivier, dressed in silk pyjamas and blue dressing gown, on a stretcher and wheeled him to a waiting Free Ambulance car. Accompanied by two hospital sisters he was sped to the Glasgow Wharf, to the rear end of the *Corinthic*, where those same workers, the object of Redington's constant fears, had rigged up a ship's derrick and sling ready to hoist him on board. Olivier laughed as, in the steady rain, the ambulance men lifted his stretcher and placed it on the canvas sling: a young girl ran forward and held an umbrella over his head. The ship's railings were lined with the Company and other passengers, in all numbering about eighty, absolutely fascinated by the spectacle: "Something happened . . . that one literally dreams about . . . up, up, and up I soared into the sky, smoothly floating over the side of the ship and gently down, as delicately as if upon an angel's wing; I landed sweetly upon the topmost deck."

They lowered him almost outside his cabin door. Here Vivien waited for him, and he greeted her with a "Good morning, Viv". He thanked the two nuns who had travelled with him from the hospital to the wharf. A moment later members of the *Corinthic*'s crew lifted him from the stretcher and carried him to his cabin. The departure, no less than the rest of the tour, took on a legendary dimension.

3 Passage Home

The role of Antigone confirmed Vivien in her absolute attachment to an ideal. A cruel play, written by a cynic playing
devil's advocate, who intensified in the attractive main role all
his defeated hope, it was a remarkably unified piece of work
for Anouilh, while in performance his stage mastery revealed
itself as it never had before.

Had Olivier's feeling about his own acting at this time been
aggressive he would, no doubt, have cast himself as Creon, a
role he could have played magnificently. But having already
Richard and Teazle in the new season, he took the much
smaller part of the Chorus. He wanted the attention, now, to
be on Vivien: he did not want to lose her and as the most
cunning interpreter and presenter of her image to the world
and therefore the spearhead of her audience, he would prove
his indispensability. He now seemed to have abandoned, in
any conventional sense, the desire to be happy with her. After
a few days' rest on board the *Corinthic* they began again to
rehearse.

At the first rehearsal Redington began a diary:

Today we read through the play twice. No mention of
movements, settings, or style to be played in. The first
reading was for alteration of one or two words, written in
the American idiom, for words more English, and also
more modern. e.g. "lots" [G.I. slang], instead we are saying
"Jimmy Riddle" which I am sure the Lord Chamberlain will
adore! Sir L. warned us of the short sentences, saying we
were used to much longer ones, however the play is well
written and on account of that we should not find it very
difficult. Sir L. began by reading his first speech as the
Chorus and from that reading we got the whole style, tone
and genre of the play. Although he read quietly and without
much expression we knew, even if we had not read the play
to ourselves, that we were going to hear of a tragedy. From
the moment he read "Antigone . . . is going to die" we
knew then, in a quiet, subtle way, the doom that was going
to over-shadow the whole play.

And that is what Sir L. said to us before we began reading

the second time. In *Oedipus* he said he had great difficulty in understanding the play and he did not really understand it by reading it nor by thinking about it, but only by feeling it. [By] Going deeper and deeper into the emotion of the play. So he suggested to us all that at the back of our minds the whole time we are playing we keep this feeling of doom. He even drew a line with hand from the top of his head to his neck about three inches from the back of his head: if you keep the feeling of doom there, he said, with the rest of your head you can feel much lighter. This, he said, will help to read some of the lines which sound rather embarrassing. Sir L. said that it was rather difficult to explain what he meant and he made it sound rather complicated, but he thought if we could try to understand it, it could help us a lot.

They had eighteen days before they reached Panama City, then three days on to Curaçao, in the Caribbean, before the final Atlantic crossing. Knowing they were on their way home at last the Company found one sure way of emotional release from the tension and fatigue of the previous months: they drank as never before, covering the whole range from beer to "unknown" cocktails: Charlie Phipps and his son, Ernie, would always be at the bar dispensing pints and ready to replenish Vivien's high-style cocktails. "Who do you think is the most sober to open the wine?" became a common cry. They no longer played "The Game" as they had on the way out. Vivien took up "Newers", the card game of Newmarket, which she played with David Kentish, Robert Beaumont, Mercia Swinburne and others. Elsie Beyer, who lived on cigarettes and coffee, fell into a deep depression: especially on the latter part of the tour there had been too little for her to do; she felt, apart from the friendships she had struck up with Eileen Beldon and with the youngest member of the stage staff, Stella Chitty, terribly isolated. During the voyage she languished moodily in her cabin, complaining of the Company's wild and scurrilous behaviour: to her annoyance Olivier seemed prepared to turn a blind eye to it—everyone needed to let their hair down, in particular the young, unmarried men for whom drink provided a safety-valve.

But the valve was not always safe, at least not entirely so in the case of Dan Cunningham and Vivien, whose drinking and flirtation on the voyage took on a new intensity. There lay Olivier in his cabin on his back, shifted bodily by deck hands into the ship's ballroom and out, trying to lay the ground work for *Antigone* and Chekhov's *The Proposal* (due, with Peter Cushing in the main role, to be played as a curtain raiser). Elsewhere, in the lounge, in the bar, in deck chairs, up on deck throwing quoits, Vivien sported with her coterie—and with her chief courtier, Dan Cunningham, who also had a leading role in *Antigone*, though Olivier had grown less and less happy with him an actor. In spite of the good notices and approval Cunningham had won in Australasia his main problem was that he could not take direction: being too nervous and lacking in experience he seemed often unable to grasp the point of what he was told. He would copy Olivier, do exactly as instructed, but somehow lacked the instinct to get it right.

Who knows if he got it right with Vivien? The past supplies neither proof nor clues. Whatever their relations he appears to have been easily discarded by Vivien and therefore in the longer term he was unimportant. Only Olivier attested that something "happened": there came a moment, he said, when on the voyage home he felt driven to have a serious talk with Vivien. He pleaded with her not to make her flirtation with one young man in the Company so obvious to the rest. "I really couldn't believe that it was justified that I should be so humiliated." If this interpretation of her behaviour is correct then she was, at this point, still putting obstacles in Cunningham's way in order to incite Olivier's pursuit of her. The result of Olivier's pleading was, to his great surprise, that

> she took it all very calmly and sweetly; she saw that she had been thoughtless and assured me that I wouldn't have cause for embarrassment any more. That was lovely, as far as it went.

But he had been left with doubt as to how far they had actually gone.

As well as *Antigone*, Vivien studied on board the role of Blanche Dubois in *Streetcar*. Since she had first received and read the script she and Larry had often discussed whether it had the dignity of true tragedy or was merely sordid. Olivier remarked how frightful and depressing he found it and when they showed it to Terence Morgan, with a view to his reading for Kowalski, Morgan was not interested. (Bonar Colleano was later cast in the role.) But they both gradually became convinced of the play's importance—placing as it did passion, or the failure of passion, in an unusually daring and modern context—and of how good a part Blanche was. The dedicatory verse of *Streetcar*, from Hart Crane's "The Broken Tower", might later have served as an epitaph on Larry's and her love:

> And so it was I entered the broken world
> To trace the visionary company of love, its voice
> An instant in the wind (I know not whither hurled)
> But not for long to hold each desperate choice.

A sculptor wrestles with stone, a writer with thought, but an actor's raw material is his own living tissue—not for the first time or the last, Olivier was fighting with his own body.

> Needless to say it was not long before I betrayed my surgeon's commands and took a liberty with the leg, which felt like solid stone; I got out of bed. When I got back in again, I thought, "I do believe I got away with it . . ."

But only moments later, as he described with unusual vividness,

> something made itself felt just above and on the inside of my patella, and tweekled downwards on its journey of two or so inches and . . . it was the pain of blood in full flood trying to get out of my knee and through the plaster . . . When . . . the ship's doctor sliced down each side of the plaster and lifted off the top half he revealed a remarkable sculpture, its shape determined by the fiercely struggling contusion seeking for *lebensraum*.

As the weather warmed up on board the *Corinthic* the crew

again erected the canvas pool: "we all swam", recalled Redington. "Vivien [was] again beautiful—suddenly swimming underwater and finding yourself alongside and touching her!" With such distinctly perceived images of cabin life dancing above the thousands of tons of refrigerated sheep carcasses in the hold they steamed towards the Panama Canal. In Panama City, where they stopped for a day, Terence Morgan had a wisdom tooth extracted and in Curaçao he and Georgina bought for their daughter Lyvia-Lee a branch of green bananas which he hoped would survive the voyage to England. In order to ripen them he tied them with string to his cabin roof.

When they crossed the time-date line someone quipped, "that was too Priestley for words"—J. B. Priestley's time plays then being in vogue—but once they met the Atlantic rough with its November storms, jokes faltered a shade as the Company turned green and life on board grew slippery and hazardous. Bernard Merefield, listening to the radio as it played "God Save the King", dutifully stood up, but when he sat down again his chair had rolled over and he landed on the floor.

In the Company's view the voyage home was a protracted leave-taking; each day one or several of them would visit Olivier in his cabin and find him in his silk pyjama jacket sitting up in bed. He would chat with them affectionately and at length: although they were to be together professionally for a further six months, the intimacy and the hero worship they felt would soon be diluted and the emotional ties blown apart. Everyone cherished the commemorative silk scarf or tie the Oliviers had given them, denoting membership of the Old Vic "family". They had won their colours, but each experienced a pang at the thought of the separation now imminent—the "family" was about to be broken up.

Nightly Vivien would appear in the dining-room looking lovely in the simplest of gowns and as she entered, according to Redington, a hush would descend as everyone turned to look at her. It was always the same: her personality dominated every gathering at which she was present. On 5 November they celebrated her thirty-fifth birthday, but without fireworks. Michael Redington wore a starched shirt with a stiff, turned-down wing collar, all he had left that was presentable:

Olivier liked it so much that he incorporated it in Redington's costume for *Antigone*.

On 16 November, beneath grey skies, they docked at Tilbury. Since Curaçao a banana from the Morgans' bunch had fallen every day: so they duly ate it. All that now remained was the black stalk.

4   London

21 January 1949. A new day in the life of the Oliviers. At 9.30 they awoke at Durham Cottage, Christchurch Street, and "smiled at each other". They breakfasted in bed on coffee and rolls, then played with the new Siamese kitten, called Boy, though for biological accuracy Vivien claimed the name should be IT. They were then driven in their hired car to the New Theatre where, in the Royal Circle Bar, they led the Company in a word rehearsal, which lasted till 1.30.

Along backstreets they crawled to the Ivy, where silence fell among the gathered celebrities as Olivier and his wife entered. He wore a camel-hair coat, she a black frock and mink. Aware how closely every movement they made was watched, they ate their light lunch: ravioli and endive salad, crème caramel.

Since their arrival back in London and as the outward image of the Company and its stars had taken over, the atmosphere had completely changed: they had become surrounded by "important people"; gone at once was that "particular friendliness you get when you have been working and playing and successful for such a long period", what Elsie called, "your pioneering, dear". The Great Lovers were back in town. Instead of being upstage about it, the Mother Country, now mindful of how her distant Dominions had fêted the pair and their Company, decided, like an elderly hen, she had to make an even greater clucking.

Lunch over, Olivier and Vivien boarded the car to do a little shopping: they still had not forgotten that two members of the Company had birthdays. Their purchases made, they drove back to Chelsea, where at 3.30 they went to bed, both dropping into sound and immediate sleep.

Precisely an hour later they awoke, had tea, chatted idly. Fifty minutes later they were again on their way to the theatre, where, in two dressing rooms facing each other at stage level, they began putting on make-up for the first night. Vivien's room smelt of flowers: carnations, lilies, roses, tulips, orchids stood in profusion everywhere. Olivier kept popping across to read out telegrams to her or to compare first night gifts. They had mementos of the tour with them even now—and they had brought back to Durham Cottage boxes of gifts of all kinds —but admirers from Australia still sent them more. As if in parody of this Olivier had introduced into *School* some new business: a cascade of bandboxes arriving at the front door as an indication of Lady Teazle's extravagances. While Vivien, having donned a blue wrap over her underwear, worked on her face, Olivier, still out of costume, vanished to wish the rest of the cast good luck.

On the previous evening, like the ghosts of Antipodean crowds, hundreds had formed outside the New even though all seats for the first night had been sold. After the dress rehearsal Olivier and Vivien, she dressed in pale-green brocade, had found themselves surrounded as they left for a party at the French Embassy: a police cordon had to be formed to enable them to board their car. The crowd yelled "Good old Larry!" Murmured he, "It's like being back in Sydney."

The opening of *The School for Scandal* passed as a great social occasion, made all the more important when everyone realised it was the first time the Oliviers had acted together on the London stage. In the front-of-house, into the flashlit foyer, the celebrities poured, "disgorged from their Rolls-Royces" (as they liked to say): Sir Ralph Richardson and his wife Meriel Forbes, Margaret Leighton, Lady Hardwicke (Sir Cedric had returned to Hollywood), Mr and Mrs David Niven, Richard Attenborough, Sir Alexander Korda and Sir Michael Balcon,

Robert Helpmann and Margot Fonteyn. Ambassadors, socialites, and government and industrial leaders also attended in force, led by the French ambassador, René Massigli, whose wife, in her Dior dress—black pearls on a black ground and with a blue sash—walked off with the fashion honours.

When the curtain rose Vivien and Olivier still had twenty minutes before their first scene. Now almost ready as Teazle, he again crossed to her dressing room, this time to give her his own present, a framed eighteenth-century drawing of a woman and a bottle of Scandale perfume. Hardly looking at them she just said "Oh darling, how lovely", slipping the bottle into her handbag. She meanwhile had taken up a packet from the table which she now gave him. In keeping with Sheridan, the present he found inside consisted of a pair of eighteenth-century cufflinks of garnets, rubies and emeralds. "For the first time together in London, the greatest actor in the world and his wife, one of the loveliest women" . . . Preceding all others to congratulate Olivier after the show was his thirteen-year-old son, Tarquin.

And so began a triumphant new season, all the more painful in its triumph because in a series of meetings with the Governors of the Old Vic, Olivier and Richardson found their arguments, that as actors they should continue to lead the Company, totally ignored. The impressive balance sheet of the tour also carried little weight, even though gross takings were £226,318, of which the British Council received £42,000 after tax and the Oliviers £5,000 as their personal share. Olivier saw to it himself that every member of the Company also got a share: "Mine's in three figures," Cushing delightedly told a friend. Thanks to its own cut, the Old Vic wiped out all its London losses and made a surplus on the 1948–9 season: but the Governors decided not to approach the Australian Government for a tax refund. A point in the minutes attributed the large profit "to the drawing power of the leading artists", to which in blue ink, Esher added, "and to the Old Vic!"*

* After leaving the Old Vic Olivier did not act for six months but went ahead with plans to expand the activities of Laurence Olivier Productions. He took out a four-year lease on the St James's Theatre, opening there in January 1950 with Christopher Fry's *Venus Observed*. Esher tried to persuade

Outside the theatre the students still queued and continued doing so for days on end, just for standing room. Indignant at being called "bobby-soxers", the student girls, dressed in scarves, sweaters and skirts, protested, "We're not . . . we don't swoon at Sinatra. And we would only do this for the Oliviers—or perhaps for Sir Ralph!" Alan Melville, the lyric writer and dramatist, wrote some verses:

> I joined the queue
> At the New
> At two
> On Wednesday afternoon.
> Me and my mum
> And a chum
> Always come,
> And we all like to get there soon.
> We hadn't a gamp;
> It was damp;
> We got cramp;
> And it's doubtful if mother will live.
> But we made cups of tea
> And we three
> All agree
> It was worth it for Larry and Viv.
>
> All Thursday passed
> Fairly fast
> And a vast
> Collection of fans joined the queue.
> Mum fainted twice;
> I'd an ice
> Which was nice;
> Though by this time we'd all got the flu.
> My friend was sick,
> But she'd pick
> Up quite quick

Olivier to work again at the Old Vic, but he refused. The Old Vic Company, in spite of having returned, in 1951, to its true home in the Waterloo Road—now repaired after extensive bomb damage—never quite regained its former glory.

Whenever we practised our cheers.
None of this marred
Our regard
For the Bard—
That is, when Sir Laurence appears.

The final stanza of Melville's verses summed up the illu-
mination supplied by the Oliviers in those drab, post-war
years when coal and food were scarce, gas flickered weakly,
and even hospitals lacked hot water—effects, according to
Winston Churchill, then Leader of the Opposition, of the
Labour Government's policy of "preaching class warfare"
and reducing England to one vast "Wormwood Scrubbery"

Upwards one plods;
Parks our bods
In the Gods:
Excitement and tension were rife.
When He appeared,
How we cheered!
Mother feared
That she'd ruptured her larynx for life.
Though I can't say
That the play
Was okay—
Old-fashioned, it all seemed to me.
At the stage-door,
The furore! . . .
And, what's more,
I *touched* him—and Vivien Leigh!

The one note of criticism of the Teazles centred around the age
Olivier gave Sir Peter. In Perth he had begun old—too
old—but in subsequent performances had been getting younger until some critics now wondered if his deeply loving but
quick-tempered manner did not upset the play in the other
direction. Surely the comedy only made sense if the needle of
Peter's jealousy pointed more towards seventy than forty.
    Why, asked Philip Hope-Wallace, should this Lady Teazle

"want to be rid of the most attractive man in town?" while
Alan Dent suggested that it was "surely more than a wee bit
perverse" of Olivier to present Sir Peter twenty years younger
than he ought to be, "just after he has startled the entire
habitable globe with a Hamlet about twenty years older than
the normal". Harold Hobson attacked his sense of style:
"Could he, the years permitting, have been witty with
Rochester, or have gambled with Fox? He would, I think,
have found Mr Allworthy a better companion, and all the
Sunday Schools in the country will say that he was right."

Most of the popular press made no effort to restrain its
praise, while even critics disliked by Olivier for underrating
Vivien's acting ability because of her beauty, were more
muted in their reservations, for example Dent who wrote that
while Vivien bewitched everyone, if she had a fault it was that
of the "first" Lady Teazle, Mrs Abington:

> her voice was of a high pitch and not very powerful. Her
> management of it alone made it an organ. Yet this was so
> perfect that we sometimes converted the mere effect into a
> cause, and supposed it was the sharpness of the tone that
> gave the sting.

Hobson felt he could not raise his question over the style here:
"Dazzled by the exquisitely fragile beauty of Miss Vivien
Leigh . . . it is impossible to consider such a problem. You
might as well try to determine, with the naked eye, whether
the sun has a corona." Ivor Brown of the *Observer* drew all the
threads together:

> It is good . . . to have the New Theatre its crowded and
> happy self once more, and especially good to welcome the
> Oliviers and their troupers, who have won a Bradmanesque
> popularity and shattered box-office records in Australia and
> New Zealand. Sir Laurence's curtain speech was a model of
> grace and I was very glad that he paid special tribute to his
> team of stage managers whose tour with three major pro-
> ductions must have been very strenuous. Stage-managers
> are what politicians call "an underprivileged section of the
> community". They don't get "notices" as a rule—and it is

not easy for those in front to realise how good or bad they are. But they can save or mar productions . . .

But Olivier had only made a passing reference in his special tribute to Cecil Beaton, who, since submitting his set and costume designs for *School* in 1947—and though receiving excellent notices for them all through 1948 and now in 1949 —had been otherwise too busy or absent to take an active interest in the production. A little after the London opening, and somewhat insensitive to just how much his lack of participation might have hurt Olivier and Vivien, Beaton went to see *School* for the first time, finding his most hopeful expectations far exceeded by the skill with which his designs had been executed, and the reverence with which they were lit. But when he dashed round backstage after the performance his reception by both the Oliviers—in particular by Vivien whom he thought of as a good friend—came as a terrible shock. Vivien did not even turn to greet him as he entered her dressing room, and while he tried to cover his embarrassment with flattery he watched her eyes of steel staring at herself, "as she rubbed a slime of dirty cold cream, a blending of rouge, eyeblack, and white foundation over her face. Not one word did she say about my contribution to the evening."

When Beaton called on Olivier he found the humiliating procedure repeated. Olivier made him sit silent in a corner of the room while he chatted to an elderly cleric, "to whom I was not introduced". Beaton never spoke again to either Vivien or Olivier.

Alan Dent's witty review of *Richard III*, which opened later on 26 January, could not praise Olivier enough. "His range of expression is extraordinary, even for him, his eyes are Machiavellian, his nose is a sinister sonnet of Baudelaire, and his hands in their scarlet gloves are quick and shrewd. He lives the life of Richard with an almost alarming gusto, and he dies the death horribly—like an earthworm cut in two." Dent applauded the Company as a whole: Peter Cushing and Terence Morgan "do far more acting as Clarence and Hastings than they do as the Surface brothers". He wrote of Vivien as Lady Anne that she had far more "strength and compulsion than I suspected were in either (a) the Lady Anne or (b) Miss Leigh". Moreover she looked almost delicious enough to eat. And for the man who might well have wanted to eat her and possibly had, Dent had a good line in back-handed praise: "Dan Cunningham looks less like a young Richmond than a young Norwegian tenor having his first shot at Tristan. But it is a very good shot."

One night during its run, in that dressing room near the stage, Vivien played Canasta, a new card game which had just caught on, and as she led, grew very excited. Olivier as Richard came off stage, according to Virginia Fairweather, in mephitic bad as opposed to mephitic good humour, and entered her dressing room, complaining of the noise. She smiled at him sweetly—everyone else was terrified—"My darling, you wouldn't hear it if you closed the door." He rocked with laughter and left—carefully closing the door behind him.★

Antigone, joining the other plays after a week, completed Olivier's demonstration of Company excellence. This time in his review Dent pointed out how Olivier had already achieved tragic greatness in *Oedipus*, but that in *Antigone* Vivien still fell short of the requirements: but Dent was possibly being unfair.

The general view turned out to be very different: Dent, like James Agate, felt you could not be tragic without a grand manner and an organ roll in the voice. Times had changed, and *Antigone*, in the skilful adaptation Anouilh had made of the Sophoclean original, itself made a good definition of the changing conditions of "the tragic".

Olivier had worked fanatically hard on the production, in particular on Vivien's voice: and she now had, as Ivor Brown confirmed, "a new and strong vocal range, a fanatical force of character, and the calm intensity of the unshakeable devotee. It is a most notable achievement and surmounts expectation." When fifteen years later Olivier came to play Othello, he knew exactly, at least partly from the experience of working with Vivien, how to lower by an octave and roughen his own voice,

★ When, in 1979, thirty-five years after being presented by John Gielgud with the sword Edmund Kean had used when playing Richard III, Olivier was asked if he would now in his turn pass on the sword, and if so to whom, he answered, "No one. It's mine."

and by this to change his personality. By this time he and Vivien had finally separated. "Cannibals" was what Olivier called the great Shakespearian roles: "Your heart and brain are pulp . . . Acting great parts devours you. It's a dangerous game."

FINISHING STROKES

A coral reef which comes short of the ocean surface is no more to the horizon than if it had never been begun, and the mere finishing stroke is what often appears to create an event which has long been potentially an accomplished thing.

Thomas Hardy, *Far From the Madding Crowd*

The union of Laurence Olivier and Vivien Leigh was the "marriage for love" of its time; its illicit beginnings were still being discussed even seven years after the ceremony, when objections to a possible knighthood for Olivier were voiced on the score that he, a clergyman's son, had hardly behaved in a respectable manner towards Leigh Holman, and had divorced his first wife.

But were he and Vivien truly married, or had both contracted themselves to passion instead, loving love itself and being in love with love—conditions they needed in order to act successfully—more than with one another? That they viewed, as far as can be judged from their actions and words, the morality of passion as the basis for marriage, when really it was only the pattern for infidelity, reveals in their attitude to love a central contradiction, responsible not only for the breakdown of their own marriage, but of countless others. Iseult is not Iseult if she loses her fugitive strangeness which so excites possession. Similarly what so entranced everyone about Vivien Leigh was that to everyone—except to Olivier once he possessed her—she had remained unobtainable. Paradoxically, to possess her meant to lose her—or that side of himself she so successfully stimulated: a sense of danger, an unfulfilled potentiality for love. Olivier, needing both of these for his acting, could never have afforded to lose either, so he could not, it would seem, have had in any conventional sense the desire to be happy with her.

The tour had made it clear to him how overstretched he could become, yet a future together could only be made by a renewal—not of the closeness between them, but of obstacle and struggle. The myth of passion, whose demands at an earlier stage they had gone through hell and torture to meet, and which had made them famous, now exacted its price—a continuation of the same kind of suffering in aid of its mystical promise.

Olivier might well have settled for less. He was now much less interested in heroic acting, and had grown more worldly and practical. He was not a womaniser, stating his opinion in his autobiography that one cannot "be more than one kind of athlete at a time", and that often "the most magnificent boxers, wrestlers, champions . . . proved to be disappointing upon the removal of that revered jock-strap". As far as he was concerned, Vivien met his desires but he did not satisfy all hers.

Vivien could not settle for less. Her extreme nature, more likely than not affected by the pain of the sacrifices made for Olivier and for her own ambition, caused her to experiment with fresh obstructions and pushed her into exploring new areas of darkness and uncertainty.

Olivier wrote sadly of the end of the tour that it was evident, "that such life as I could offer to Vivien at this time was dull in the extreme". Dullness, boredom? To any ordinary being the tour could have been something very different but the operative words are "to Vivien". All that was perhaps left to her was to enter that broken world adumbrated in Hart Crane's poem; who better to introduce her to it than Blanche Dubois?

Peter Finch and his wife Tamara arrived in London from Australia on 17 November 1948 and a short time after were invited round to Durham Cottage for drinks, while in March 1949 Laurence Olivier Productions successfully presented Finch in James Bridie's *Daphne Laureola* in the part of Ernest Piaste, the Viennese lover. Vivien became attracted to Finch, while her apparent determination to foster him as a substitute for Olivier promoted the conflict and excitement that Finch found unable to resist. As she had once been Olivier's protégée so now did Finch become hers, later saying, "Of all the women I loved, Vivien had the mind, style and wit to match her beauty."

But one day in the spring of 1949, before her affair with Finch began, Vivien informed Olivier that she did not love him any more. She disclosed this in the small winter-garden of the porch at Durham Cottage, after they had finished lunch. Her words acted on him "like a candle-snuffer": he would jokily complain later, at odd moments, "I lorst you in Australia"—yet both he and she knew that without his help she could never have succeeded later that year as Blanche Dubois in *A Streetcar Named Desire*.

Tennessee Williams said of Blanche, "She was a demonic creature, the size of her feeling was too great for her to contain without the escape to madness." As director of *Streetcar* Olivier not only steered the production through all the practical and technical problems that arose during rehearsal—including a brush with the Lord Chamberlain's office over its refusal to allow Blanche to describe her dead young husband as homosexual—but he grasped at once the central difficulty the role presented to Vivien. He had noticed how, by altering one feature, one could make a whole new face: now, by pushing Vivien to adopt an even deeper and rougher voice than she had in *Antigone*, he helped her to achieve a complete change of personality. It was Vivien's shortcoming that she did not see that Olivier's transforming power over her acting was how, for him, love expressed itself.

But it never crossed Olivier's mind to think that, on a personal level, Blanche Dubois could be bad for Vivien. Olivier could always shrug off the part to which, while he was playing it, his commitment remained total. She had not, as he well knew, the same capacity to throw herself into a part as he did: something blocked her—her immaturity as an artist, perhaps, or that "primitive passport" of her looks, as Edith Evans had called it—from releasing with safety her whole sexual and emotional energy; nor had motherhood developed a broadness and stability of character which gave her psychological balance and extra resources for her art: hence she did not really understand Olivier when he put his whole force into playing a part and running a company.*

* When Vivien and Olivier acted in *Antony and Cleopatra* at the St James's Theatre in 1951, Kenneth Tynan attacked Olivier for subduing his "blow-like ebullience to match her. Blunting his iron precision, levelling away his

"I have found that although actors can play any part and shake it off, actresses cannot," commented Alan Dent when Vivien passed him a copy of *Streetcar* to read: she called him "impossible". Greta Garbo had already turned down Tennessee Williams's personal request to play Blanche in the film on the grounds that she could "never be an involved and complicated person: I'm too direct and masculine. I couldn't bear to tell lies, and see things round corners, like that girl." So it was courageous of Vivien to take Blanche on and by doing this turn her back on the more romantic heroines with which she had up to then been identified. She must have known that she risked, by portraying Blanche's rape and madness, giving the audience nothing less than a kick in the stomach: "low and repugnant" was how an MP described it in the House of Commons, while *The Times* concluded that the purpose of the play was "to reveal a prostitute's past in her present".

Playing Blanche did get inside Vivien, confusing her grasp over the reality of herself, and she could not shake Blanche off after she had ceased playing her; she did not possess the self-control and the artistic discipline needed to handle the elements of hysteria she could find within herself. Playing her became a form of suicide:

> I challenge any woman [she told David Lewin in an interview] to be able to accept the scene when [Blanche's] face is held pitilessly under a naked light bulb and she is asked to contemplate what she will look like when her beauty has gone. Blanche is a woman with everything stripped away: she is a tragic figure and I understand her. But playing her tipped me into madness.

She took to drinking more heavily than before. As the underlying guilt over her first marriage—her equivalent of Blanche's loneliness in the play—sought a more pronounced outlet, so she had, it was widely believed, several one-night

---

towering authority, he meets her halfway". Tynan emphasised how much Olivier's acting was a form of love-making: "You cannot act by instalments, and Olivier's relationship with his audience is that of a skilled but tantalizing lover."

affairs. But Olivier continued as her mentor throughout the successful run; later, on the strength of her stage performance, she played Blanche in the Hollywood film version which won her an Academy Award, and which established the reputation of Marlon Brando, who played Kowalski.

Sometime later, in 1953, when, as passengers on a small French freighter travelling from America's West Coast the long way home through Panama and Curaçao, Vivien and Olivier found themselves truly alone again they had nothing to say: "The stark reality of our own company," Olivier wrote, "plunged us both into deep depression . . . We had never before been made to face the extent to which our lives together had been supported and bolstered up by the companionship of our friends and the glitter of our position." Neither of them was now able to provide for the other that strength of position they had once enjoyed with their respective first spouses. While Olivier's depression almost exactly repeated what he had felt with Jill Esmond in 1932: "We badly needed characters in our lives; we had precious little to make conversation about otherwise."

Vivien had no real desire to escape the ultimate consequences of her uncompromising attitude towards passion. Given her spontaneity which she sought always to maintain, her marriage to Olivier now became the negation of passion, while the passion itself could no longer disguise what it hid: an egocentric seeking of experience to the bitter end, in short, a desire for death. While this may have been largely repressed in her conscious, everyday life she nevertheless did choose these consequences and her manic-depressive illness was but one expression of the death wish, and therefore of her original desire for, and commitment to, passion. She herself said no less: "I don't pretend and I am prepared to accept the consequences of my action."

The pace of her deterioration had quickened from 1951 onwards: having admired her exquisite beauty in Sydney in 1948, Beryl Graham, a biology teacher from Wollstonecraft, New South Wales, found herself "all the more shocked when I saw her at arm's length in London, in 1953, just after one of her periods of illness and its ravage on her face". Her affairs with

Peter Finch and others highlighted her decline, as did the excesses of her behaviour during depression. In particular, during the filming of *Elephant Walk* with Finch in Ceylon she broke down and started reciting long sections from *Streetcar*: a little later, in Hollywood, Olivier, summoned to take her home, discovered her stark naked balancing on a baluster rail. Olivier found that he could not seriously blame Finch who only did to him what he had done to Leigh Holman seventeen years before.

But as she suffered more, becoming in the process more completely estranged from Olivier, so did she try as much as she could to punish him and try to pass on to him as much of the pain as she could. Curiously enough he remained detached, "self-removing" as he termed it, finding her more and more changed, until he could console himself that she was no longer the same girl he had fallen in love with, and that therefore he was justified in loving her "that much less". Again the Machiavellian streak of practicality directed his feeling, though once he did try, as he put it, "fucking" their love back into existence: this worked no better than the pregnancy she underwent in 1956, when aged forty-two, which finally, and by then almost inevitably, miscarried.

"Larry boy runs from the truth because he cannot face it. He finds making contact difficult," Vivien said of him, but she fought ruthlessly against any plans he suggested for their separation. When, in 1959, he admitted that he now loved someone else she tried, for nights on end, to deny him sleep. Seeing him drift off one night she grabbed a wet flannel and slashed him across the eyes with it, and when he retired to another room she followed him, beginning to hammer on the door in such a way that he thought she would never stop. Then something inside him snapped. Throwing open the door he grabbed her wrists, dragged her along the passage, pushed open her door and, in "all-possessing rage", hurled her across the room to the bed. As he wrote,

> Before hitting the bed she struck the outside corner of her left eyebrow on the corner of her marble bedside table top, opening up a wound half an inch from her temple and half an inch from her eye.

In June 1967, eight years after her separation from Olivier, Vivien fought a further and sudden worsening of tuberculosis, which had now spread to both her lungs. She refused to go to hospital, and failed to stop smoking as ordered, not even heeding the advice of her doctor against getting up and moving about her room if alone. A few nights later she fell down on the floor of her bedroom, coughing and choking till she died.

Olivier, himself undergoing treatment in hospital for cancer of the prostate, was summoned the following morning to her flat where he found she had been placed back on the bed. He noticed on the floor the hastily cleaned up mess, later commenting, "a cruel stroke of fate to deliver that particular little death-blow to one so scrupulously dainty".

To disguise his feelings from those present he moved around the bedroom, picking up small objects, some of which had once been his, remarking in a matter-of-fact way on them, withdrawing himself yet again in an apparently tasteless manner into technicalities. When the undertakers arrived to lay out the body for the coffin he wanted to remain behind and watch, and finally had to be persuaded to leave.

After a private Roman Catholic Mass in a chapel in Cadogan Street and the cremation ceremony at Golders Green, Cecil Tennant, Olivier's and Vivien's oldest friend and partner —trusted by Olivier, he had once lain all night, fully clothed, on a bed beside Vivien, holding her to calm her down—drove off in a new sports-car to collect his children. On the way home the steering column of the car broke, and it went off the road, hitting a tree, killing Tennant instantly. When informed by telephone Olivier, gasping with the shock, cried out, "Boy, what have we done?"

★ ★ ★

"You can reach a point," reflected Olivier many years later on his and Vivien's final parting, "when it's like a life-raft that can hold only so many. You cast away the hand grasping. You let it go. You do not take it on board because otherwise it's both of you. Two instead of one.

"Then you go on living and there you are, with it, knowing what has happened, remembering its details . . ."

APPENDICES

APPENDIX I

THE COMPANY

LAURENCE OLIVIER   VIVIEN LEIGH
GEORGE RELPH

EILEEN BELDON	MERCIA SWINBURNE
TERENCE MORGAN	PETER CUSHING
DAN CUNNINGHAM	BERNARD MEREFIELD
HUGH STEWART	ROBERT BEAUMONT
JAMES BAILEY	THOMAS HEATHCOTE
PEGGY SIMPSON	MEG MAXWELL
GEORGINA JUMEL	ANNE McGRATH
HELEN BECK	JOHN BARNARD
GEORGE COOPER	TONY GAVIN
OLIVER HUNTER	DENIS LEHRER
DERRICK PENLEY	MICHAEL REDINGTON

JANE SHIRLEY

STAGE STAFF

General Manager	ELSIE BEYER
Company Manager	CLIVE WOODS
Stage Director	DAVID KENTISH
Stage Managers	DOUGLAS MURCHIE
	ROY HAWKINS
Assistant Stage	JANE SHIRLEY
Managers	STELLA CHITTY
Master Carpenter	CHARLES PHIPPS
Chief Electrician	WILLIAM BUNDY
Property Master	EARNEST PHIPPS
Wardrobe Mistress	EMMA SELBY-WALKER
Master Painter and	
Head Flyman	ROGER RAMSDELL

APPENDIX II

CAST LISTS OF THE PLAYS

THE SCHOOL FOR SCANDAL

1st Servant at Lady Sneerwell's	TONY GAVIN
2nd Servant at Lady Sneerwell's	ROBERT BEAUMONT
Lady Sneerwell	MERCIA SWINBURNE
Snake	OLIVER HUNTER
Joseph Surface	PETER CUSHING
Maria	PEGGY SIMPSON
Mrs. Candour	EILEEN BELDON
Crabtree	BERNARD MEREFIELD
Sir Benjamin Backbite	DAN CUNNINGHAM
Sir Peter Teazle	LAURENCE OLIVIER
Rowley	HUGH STEWART
1st Servant at the Teazles'	THOMAS HEATHCOTE
2nd Servant at the Teazles'	GEORGE COOPER
Lady Teazle's Maid	MEG MAXWELL
Lady Teazle	VIVIEN LEIGH
Sir Oliver Surface	GEORGE RELPH
Moses	JAMES BAILEY
Trip, Servant at Charles Surface's	ROBERT BEAUMONT
2nd Servant at Charles Surface's	OLIVER HUNTER
Charles Surface	TERENCE MORGAN
Sir Harry Bumper	TONY GAVIN
Careless	THOMAS HEATHCOTE
Sir Toby	GEORGE COOPER

William, Servant at Joseph Surface's	GEORGE COOPER

The Play Produced by LAURENCE OLIVIER

Scenery and Costumes by CECIL BEATON

The Orchestra under the Direction of HAROLD INGRAM

Music derived from *The Great Elopement*,
HANDEL-BEECHAM
for which grateful acknowledgments are extended to
SIR THOMAS BEECHAM, BART.

Dance Arranged by Andrée Howard

RICHARD III

King Edward IV	BERNARD MEREFIELD
Queen Elizabeth, his wife	MERCIA SWINBURNE

George, Duke of
    Clarence, brother to
    the King
	PETER CUSHING

Richard, Duke of
    Gloster, brother to
    the King, afterwards
    King Richard III
	LAURENCE OLIVIER

Duchess of York, mother to the King	MEG MAXWELL
Lord Hastings, friend to the King	TERENCE MORGAN
Jane Shore, mistress to the King	JANE SHIRLEY
Prince of Wales Sons to the King	ANNE McGRATH
Duke of York by Elizabeth	PEGGY SIMPSON

Lady Anne,
    daughter-in-law
    of Henry VI,
    afterwards wife
    of Richard III
	VIVIEN LEIGH

177

Margaret of Anjou,
  widow of King
  Henry VI   EILEEN BELDON
Duke of Buckingham   GEORGE RELPH
Sir William Catesby   ROBERT BEAUMONT
Sir Richard Ratcliffe   of Gloster's   OLIVER HUNTER
Lord Lovel   faction   DERRICK PENLEY
Lord Rivers, brother
  to Elizabeth   of the   JAMES BAILEY
Marquis of   Queen's   TONY GAVIN
  Dorset   Sons to   faction
Lord Grey   Elizabeth   DENIS LEHRER
Lord Stanley,
  Earl of Derby   HUGH STEWART
Cardinal Bouchier,
  Archbishop of
  Canterbury   PETER CUSHING
John Morton,
  Bishop of Ely   BERNARD MEREFIELD
Lord Mayor of London   THOMAS HEATHCOTE
Brackenbury,
  Lieutenant of
  the Tower   GEORGE COOPER
Two Murderers,   OLIVER HUNTER,
  hired by Gloster   THOMAS HEATHCOTE
A Messenger   DENIS LEHRER
A Priest   DAN CUNNINGHAM
Sir James Tyrrell   JAMES BAILEY
Earl of Richmond,
  afterwards
  King Henry VII   DAN CUNNINGHAM
Captain Blount   Friends to   BERNARD MEREFIELD
Earl of Oxford   Richmond   TONY GAVIN
Sir William Brandon   THOMAS HEATHCOTE
Citizens, Monks, Attendants, Guards, Messengers, Soldiers,
etc. GEORGINA JUMEL,
ANNE McGRATH, JANE SHIRLEY,
PEGGY SIMPSON, JAMES BAILEY,
JOHN BARNARD, ROBERT BEAUMONT,
GEORGE COOPER, THOMAS HEATHCOTE,

OLIVER HUNTER, DENIS LEHRER,
DERRICK PENLEY, MICHAEL REDINGTON.

The Play Produced by JOHN BURRELL

Scenery by Morris Kestleman
Costumes by Doris Zinkeisen

Music by Herbert Menges

The Orchestra under the Direction of HAROLD INGRAM

Fight arranged by Peter Copley   Lighting by John Sullivan

THE SKIN OF OUR TEETH

News Commentator	DAN CUNNINGHAM
Sabina	VIVIEN LEIGH
Mr Fitzpatrick	GEORGE RELPH
Mrs Antrobus	EILEEN BELDON
Dinosaur	DENIS LEHRER
Mammoth	ANNE McGRATH
Telegraph Boy	THOMAS HEATHCOTE
Henry	TERENCE MORGAN
Gladys	GEORGINA JUMEL
Mr Antrobus	LAURENCE OLIVIER
Doctor	BERNARD MEREFIELD
Professor	PETER CUSHING
Judge	HUGH STEWART
Homer	OLIVER HUNTER
Miss E. Muse	MEG MAXWELL
Miss T. Muse	HELEN BECK
Miss M. Muse	PEGGY SIMPSON
1st Usher	DERRICK PENLEY
2nd Usher	MICHAEL REDINGTON
American Announcer	ROBERT BEAUMONT
Majorettes	ANNE McGRATH, JANE SHIRLEY, HELEN BECK
Fortune Teller	MERCIA SWINBURNE
Chair Pushers	GEORGE COOPER, JOHN BARNARD

Negro Chair Pusher	JAMES BAILEY
Defeated Candidate	BERNARD MEREFIELD
Conveners	HUGH STEWART,
	DENIS LEHRER,
	THOMAS HEATHCOTE,
	TONY GAVIN,
	OLIVER HUNTER,
	PETER CUSHING
Old Lady	MEG MAXWELL
Mr Tremayne	BERNARD MEREFIELD
Hester	MEG MAXWELL
Ivy	PEGGY SIMPSON

Produced by LAURENCE OLIVIER

Decor by ROGER FURSE
Music by ANTHONY HOPKINS

The Orchestra under the Direction of HAROLD INGRAM

ACT I	The Ice
ACT II	The Deluge
ACT III	The Reconstruction

Sources

Following are those autobiographies or memoirs on which I have drawn most frequently (place of publication is London unless otherwise indicated).

James Agate, *Ego* (9 vols., 1935–48: vol. 1, Hamish Hamilton, 1935; vol. 2, Gollancz, 1936; vols. 3–9, Harrap, 1938-48)
  Brief Chronicles (Cape, 1943)
  Red Letter Nights (Cape, 1944)
Felix Barker, *The Oliviers* (Hamish Hamilton, 1953)
Cecil Beaton, *The Happy Years* 1944–48 (Weidenfeld and Nicolson, 1972)
  The Strenuous Years 1948–1955 (Weidenfeld and Nicolson, 1973)
Denys Blakelock, *Advice to a Player* (Heinemann, 1957)
  Round the Next Corner (Gollancz, 1967)
Ivor Brown, *The Way of My World* (Collins, 1954)
Hal Burton (ed.), *Great Acting* (BBC Publications, 1967)
  (ed.), *Acting in the Sixties* (BBC Publications, 1970)
Crisp, *Ben Chifley* (Longmans, 1963)
Alan Dent, *Vivien Leigh: A Bouquet* (Hamish Hamilton, 1969)
Fabia Drake, *Blind Fortune* (Kimber, 1978)
Elaine Dundy, *Finch, Bloody Finch* (Michael Joseph, 1980)
Anne Edwards, *Vivien Leigh* (W. H. Allen, 1977)
Virginia Fairweather, *Cry God for Larry* (Calder, 1969)
Trader Faulkner, *Peter Finch* (Angus and Robertson, 1979)
Yolande Finch, *Finchy* (Arrow, 1980)
James Forsyth, *Tyrone Guthrie* (Hamish Hamilton, 1976)
Logan Gourlay (ed.), *Olivier* (Weidenfeld and Nicolson, 1973)
Tyrone Guthrie, *A Life in the Theatre* (Hamish Hamilton, 1960)
Thomas Kiernan, *Olivier* (Sidgwick and Jackson, 1981)
Michael Korda, *Charmed Lives* (Harmondsworth: Penguin Books, 1980)
Karol Kulik, *Alexander Korda* (W. H. Allen, 1975)
Charles Landstone, *Off-stage* (Elek, 1949)

Jesse L. Lasky, Jr. (with Pat Silver), *Love Scene* (Brighton: Angus and Robertson, 1978)

Margaret Morley (ed.), *Olivier: The Films and Faces* (LSP, 1978)

Nora Nicholson, *Chameleon's Dish* (Elek, 1973)

Cynthia Nolan, *Outback: A Journey Across Australia* (Methuen, 1949)

    Paradise, and Yet (Macmillan, 1971)

Laurence Olivier, *Confessions of an Actor* (Weidenfeld and Nicolson, 1982)

Leslie Rees, *The Making of Australian Drama* (Sydney: Angus and Robertson, 1973)

    Towards an Australian Drama (Sydney: Angus and Robertson, 1953)

Paul Tabori, *Alexander Korda* (Oldbourne, 1959)

Laurence Thompson, *Behind the Curtain* (Ward Lock, 1951)

Kenneth Tynan, *He That Plays the King* (Longmans, 1950)

    Curtains (Longmans, 1961)

    The Sound of Two Hands Clapping (Cape, 1975)

    A View of the English Stage (Paladin, 1976)

John Vickers, *The Old Vic in Photographs* (Saturn, 1947)

    Five Seasons (Saturn, 1950)

E. G. Harcourt Williams, *Four Years at the Old Vic 1929–1933* (Putnam, 1935)

    Old Vic Saga (Winchester, 1949)

Audrey Williamson, *Old Vic Drama* (Rockliff, 1951)

    Theatre of Two Decades (Rockliff, 1951)

I am grateful to the editors of and contributors to the following newspapers (London and elsewhere) and magazines in which I have consulted articles, reviews, etc.:
Advertizer (Adelaide), *The Age* (Melbourne), *The Argus* (Melbourne), *Auckland Star*, *Australian Woman's Weekly*, *Birmingham Post*, *Courier Mail* (Brisbane), *Daily Express*, *Daily Herald*, *Daily Mail*, *Daily Mirror* (Sydney), *Daily News* (Adelaide), *Daily News* (Perth), *Daily Telegraph* (Sydney), *The Dominion* (Wellington), *Evening News*, *Evening Standard*, *Evening Star* (Dunedin), *The Herald* (Melbourne), *Manchester Guardian*, *Mercury* (Hobart), *New Statesman*, *New York Times*, *New Zealand Herald*, *Observer*, *Otago Daily Times* (Dunedin), *Spectator*,

Sources

Sun-News Pictorial (Melbourne), *Sunday Mail* (Brisbane), *Sunday Times*, *Sunday Times* (Perth), *Sydney Morning Herald*, *Sydney Sun and Guardian*, *Sydney Sunday Telegraph*, *Telegraph* (Brisbane), *The Times*, *Truth* (Brisbane), *Truth* (Sydney), *West Australian* (Perth).

Acknowledgments

I thank the following for consenting to be interviewed, for sending or collecting information, and for kindness or help in one or more of innumerable other ways. The late Sir Ralph Richardson once commented that what struck him forcibly on a visit to Australia and New Zealand was something "of which the atlas gave no hint, namely that the Australians and New Zealanders thought a great deal about us in Great Britain, a great deal more, I should say, than we think about them". My list, as far as is possible, shows where the mentioned were in 1948.

PERSONNEL OF THE TOUR (AND RELATIONS)

John Barnard, Eileen Beldon, Floy Bell, Bill Bundy, Margaret Burrell, Peter Copley, Peter Cushing, Patrick Donnel, Kate Griffin, Thomas Heathcote, Peter Hiley, Pat Legh, Brian Jones, Georgina Jumel, Terence Morgan, Sir Laurence Olivier, Michael Redington, Mercia Swinburne, Dorothy Welford.

WESTERN AUSTRALIA

S. C. Anderson (Mrs), Norma Bundell, Jennifer Gillett, Sandra Gorringe, Kay Jackson, M. W. Jarvis, K. T. Johnson, Maurice Jones, Ivan King, Mollie Lyon, Edna McNamara, Shirley McWhirter, R. A. Yelland.

SOUTH AUSTRALIA

Elaine Barker, Judith Brown, J. Chapman (Mrs), Jean M. Cook, Ian Davidson, Betty Fisher, Sue Heyson, Betty and Ray Hill, Dorothy Kimber, Pat McDonald, Joan Osman, Jo Peoples, Constance Radcliffe, The Most Revd T. T. Reed, Jean Rice, Keith Rosenthal, Marie Simonis, Gillian Thomas, Lois Thompson, Betty Treagus, Catherine Veitch.

Acknowledgments

VICTORIA

Isabel Black, Pamela Bolles, Betty Bone, Margaret Buncle, Douglas Calder, Margaret Calder, Patricia Carver, Nancy Dinsmore, Sadie Enright, Paul Farmer, Shirley Fraser, Pam George, Veronica Hopper, Ray Kennedy, Terry King, Lois Kinson, Hattie Laver, Joan Mawson, Alma Nelson, Rosemary Robertson (Canberra), Mimi Roennfeldt, Gwendoline Rose, Joan Sheedy.

TASMANIA

Claire Davis, G. A. Davis (Mrs), Lesley Morgan, Michael Roe, Judith Stump.

NEW SOUTH WALES

Isabel Andrews, Wilmore Bakewell, Michael Bolloten, Sister Philomena Bonnington, T. Essington Breen, James Carroll, J. M. Chambers (Mrs), Dr P. L. Cunningham, Anne Fenwick, Gerald Fischer, Jan French, John Gardiner, Ethel Gibb, Kath Gilchrist, Frances Gleeson, Beryl Graham, Walter Hartley, Betty Harvey, C. E. Haymet (Mrs), Margaret Hunter, J. E. Israel, J. W. Jackson, Joy Kay, Tom Lake, Sydney Levine, Anne Marshall, K. Marshall (Mrs), Margot McGrath, Andrew McKinnon, Jean Mitchell, Wendy Moore, Robert Moylan, Helen Page, Nancy Parrott, Rosemary Robertson, Milton L. Rumble, Felicia Smith, Leila Williams, Georgina Worth.

QUEENSLAND

Denise Arnold, Daphne Benham, Delys Carver, Anne Shaw Chandler, Dorothy Crawley, Beryl Harris, Patricia Kiefel, Grace Lynch, Gwenda Prewett, B. L. Thompson, Rita Watson, Morris and Vi Williams.

NEW ZEALAND

H. Anderson, Isobel Andrews, Gertrude Bailey, Elaine Barton, Maureen Campbell, Angela Caughey, Betty Curnow, Pam Deans, John Enror, Brian Fisher, Betty Fletcher, Cynthia Fletcher, M. Graham (Mrs), Rae Innes, Hugh Janson, Bev Key, M. M. MacFarlane (Mrs), P. J. MacGregor (Mrs), Doreen McKay, Douglas McYawan, Dorothy Moses, Bar-

bara Packwood, June Parker, W. H. Pearson, Shirley Pidding-
ton, Sister Mary Quittenden, Joyce Rogers, Henry Rollet, W.
R. Saljko, Joan Sellors, Shirley Simmons, Mona Smith, Joan
Smyth, Nancy Steer, Revd D. W. Storkey, Victor Thom,
Margaret Thompson, Joan Tibble, Charles Walker, Murray
Wilson, Iris Winchester.

I am deeply grateful to Michael Redington for his permission
to quote from the letters he wrote to Jack and Winifred Keates
and which after their deaths were found intact and returned to
him; to Lord Olivier for his permission to quote from unpub-
lished letters to John Burrell on pp. 50–51, 54, 78–9, 103,
115–16; to the late Alan Melville, for the verses on pp. 159–60,
to Kate Griffin for her collection of Old Vic material, and to
Margaret Burrell for letting me consult the late John Burrell's
papers. Thanks are also due to Colin Benham and the Governors of the Old Vic for giving me permission to consult their
archives. My special gratitude is due to Pamela Deans of Tara,
Coalgate, New Zealand, for sending me the scrapbook of the
tour in her possession, compiled by her niece, Marie Donaldson. The journal kept by Olivier for the early part of the tour
was first published in Felix Barker's *The Oliviers* (Hamish
Hamilton, 1953). I have endeavoured to contact holders of
copyright in the illustrations and regret any omissions.

Much kindness has been shown me by the staff of the
following libraries and institutions where I have worked:
Australia House, BBC (Sound and Written) Archives, BBC
Television Centre, British Film Institute, Colindale Newspaper Library, Bodleian Library, Oxford; Central Library,
Westgate, Oxford; Rhodes House Library, Oxford. In particular I thank Morag Robinson, John Bright-Holmes, and Ion
Trewin at Hodder and Stoughton. For reading the draft text I
thank Catharine Carver, Linda Kelly, J. C. Trewin, Robyn
Wallis, and B. A. Young. Lastly, I thank Linda Rowley for
typing the manuscript. I must add that the interpretations I
place on the events and characters which I describe, or material
I include, are wholly my own.

G.O'C.

Oxford
September 1983

INDEX

Index

Index

Index

Index

Index